Overcoming loneliness together

A Christian Approach

Overcoming loneliness together

A Christian Approach

Mary Alban Bouchard, CSJ

NOVALIS

Cover design: Denis De Carufel

Drawings: Toby McGivern, OMI

Layout: Gilles Lépine

Photo (back cover): Anthony Vecera

© 1991 Novalis, Saint Paul University, Ottawa

Novalis
P.O. Box 990, Outremont, P.Q. H2V 4S7

Legal deposit: 1st trimester, 1991
  National Library of Canada
  Bibliothèque nationale du Québec

ISBN: 2-89088-479-1

Printed in Canada

Canadian Cataloguing in Publication Data

Bouchard, Mary Alban
  Overcoming loneliness together

Includes bibliographical references.
ISBN 2-89088-479-1

  1. Loneliness. 2. Loneliness--Religious aspects--
Christianity. I. Title.

BV4911.B69 1991   155.9'2   C90-090555-7

NOVALIS

Contents

Introduction 7
Loneliness in general 11
Being young is not easy 21
Alone in my wheelchair 35
The loneliness of the long-distance runner 59
The loneliness of culture shock 71
Bottled loneliness 89
Alienation: The lonely psyche 109
Dying and living with loneliness 141
Sentenced to loneliness 161
The loneliness of separation 175
The loneliness of "Religion" 201
The loneliness of age 227
Friendship and loneliness 251
Universal loneliness, universal communion 265
Notes 277
Bibliography 281

Introduction

Several good books have been written on loneliness. Some of these I have read. Paula Ripple's *Walking With Loneliness* is psychologically upbuilding with remedies for loneliness. Father Ron Rolheiser's *The Loneliness Factor* is a thorough but very human theological analysis. David Reisman's *The Lonely Crowd* touches on the cultural phenomenon of loneliness. Dorothy Day's *The Long Loneliness* is frankly autobiographical.

Why then another book on loneliness? Why this book?

The inspiration for this book came from reader responses to a "Special Section" in *Living With Christ* on the topic of loneliness. It was a reprint of *Christopher Notes*.* Judging from the number of letters to the editor, it touched many people where they experienced loneliness. The *Notes* listed first some of the feelings associated with loneliness: alone in a crowd, abandoned, rejected, misunderstood, isolated, uncertain, afraid. They went on to recommend: accept, go into, go through, let go of loneliness. *Overcoming loneliness together* takes up from that "Special Section" and the responses to it, and tries to answer the question of the little boy quoted there. This little boy had no one to play with and so asked God: "Can you help me become unlonely?"

The method used in this book is neither philosophical nor theological, psychological nor sociological, though it is all of these in some way. Rather it is simply human: it tells people's stories—stories of their experienced loneliness and what they did with it, stories told to me or told from my own observations or experience. I am convinced that telling the stories of courage of the persons interviewed and their positive, largely successful, efforts to cope with loneliness is the best help I can offer to readers.

These stories represent people of various circumstances. They express many kinds of loneliness. In asking people to tell me their story so that you, the readers, might benefit from them, I soon realized I was touching some holy places. I was asking people to remember their pain. I tried to tread gently. People were generous in speaking with me so that I might write this book for others. I was both surprised and edified by this generosity.

So before you read on, join with me in thanking those who have really written this book with me. Join me in thanking God for the human spirit that reaches out for life in the midst of this mysterious thing we call loneliness and goes on to walk with others in their time of loneliness.

This book postulates that everyone experiences loneliness. All human beings know what it is. It is universal. Yet, each experience is unique and particular, and that makes the person feel all the more lonely and alone. Hearing a person's story or seeing the images by which another person captures the experience of loneliness, we get in touch with our own. At the same moment, we realize we are not alone in our loneliness. We are, after all, human like everyone else. And maybe there is even something positive about the experience of loneliness. Maybe it contains a truth that can set us free.

The format of the book is simple. The first chapter presents human loneliness in general. Each of the following eleven chapters includes four features: 1. introductory remarks to orient the chapter and the kind of loneliness it discusses; 2. people's stories with some comments by the author and interviewer; 3. scriptural reflections delving into the biblical story, so that we may find consolation and place our own loneliness in the human story within the context of the divine story; 4. a summary of helps gathered from the chapter to lessen our loneliness.

The second last chapter is about friendship, a subject so closely related to that of loneliness, and a subject of interest to persons in all walks of life. The final chapter is one of concluding, if not conclusive, reflections by the author on the loneliness we share.

Loneliness in general

Loneliness seems to have become a phenomenon in highly industrialized, highly "civilized" cultures. Why? Because in general these lose touch with the earth itself and with the life processes of birth, growth and death. We surround ourselves with concrete which is very cold and very lonely indeed. We immerse ourselves in things that separate us from other people: cars, home computer businesses, computer games or apartments and anonymity.

Canada in particular suffers from this phenomenon: we are a very large country whose geography and climate make us somewhat lonely people. In addition, cinema and television have made us people who sit in the dark a good deal and do not speak.

Loneliness, temporary or chronic, has been described in a variety of ways: gnawing, empty, abandoned, bereft, no place to go, deserted, lost, unknown, totally insignificant, isolated, alienated, homesick, dislocated, without meaning, void, absent, desolate, vaguely anxious, no one knows where I am and no one cares, not understood. One phrase that might well describe the sense of it is the title of one of Timothy Findley's books: *Not Wanted On The Voyage*. Some of the above adjectives are the same as those used to describe anxiety itself, that anxiety which psychologist Rollo May calls "the most painful emotion to which the human animal is heir."[1] The word "heir" connotes an inherited condition.

Some of the physical feelings accompanying loneliness are similar to those describing anxiety: constriction in the chest, hollow feeling in the pit of the stomach, vague bewilderment. The feeling is like that of a child who realizes he is lost, while grown-ups try not to panic. All humans know the feeling. All long for something and someone familiar and claspable, never to be lost. But who can provide imperishability and who will guarantee even perishable satisfaction for that deep human ache? Only the One who is life and love both.

Loneliness in lyric and literature

Many songs express human loneliness in poignant ways: "The Streets of London," "You Needed Me," "Yesterday's Dreams," "Are You Going Away?" "Solitaire," "Memories." Some songs—"Country Road," "Blue Bayou," "Gloccamorra"—express nostalgia or the homesickness version of loneliness. The chorus of "The Streets of London" asks:

> "So how can you tell me you're lonely
> And say for you the sun don't shine?
> Let me take you by the hand
> And lead you through the streets of London.
> I'll show you something to make you
> change your mind."

This chorus may hold the clue to a cure for the general disease, as do the words of "You Needed Me" and "Memories" from *Cats*: "Touch me! It's so easy to leave me all alone with the memory... If you touch me you'll understand what happiness is. Look! a new day has begun."

Great literature in any and every language has portrayed the deeply basic loneliness of the human journey, particularly in the great epics. The story is repeated in the solitary underground journey of the hero or heroine. The journey is perilous and the task seemingly impossible for a human to carry out. In the end, however, a great new life is achieved, if not for the individual, certainly for the race.

Think, for example, of the wanderings of Homer's Ulysses separated from his dear Penelope; Virgil's Aeneas fleeing Troy but finally becoming the founder of Rome; Jason seeking the Golden Fleece to gain his inheritance; Beowulf of Anglo-Saxon heroism who sought alone the monster of the lake; Dante in the journey to the Inferno, Purgatorio and, at last, the Paradiso; Galahad seeking the Holy Grail; Psyche who was required to go to the underworld to bring back beauty; Orpheus who sought his wife Eurydice in the depths and was not able to bring her back; Gilgamesh of the ancient Mesopotamian epic, who also had to embark on the same sort of journey. It is the well-known yet lonely and difficult undertaking of life.

Loneliness in the spiritual life

This is seen again in the stories of Abraham, Jacob, Joseph, Daniel, Ruth, the Exodus through the desert, and the Exile to Babylon where the people wept on the banks of the river and hung up their harps, so homesick were they for Jerusalem. We find the same theme in the spiritual journeys described and lived by John of the Cross and Teresa of Avila (whose fifth mansion is through a terrible underground passage), in Thomas Merton's life and search. While these were writing of the spiritual life, one cannot separate the spiritual from the human journey, the journey to wholeness which is the task of every person.

Carl Gustav Jung, though I believe he remained in the realm of the psychological and did not move into the realm of faith, taught and wrote of the journey or process of "individuation" in which the person becomes integrated, mature and identified. It is the journey within and has been called the longest journey. It is one that we fear because we fear our own darkness and because we must go alone, though not without helps. Those who have gone on it can advise and assure those who are on their way.

We cannot fail to include the journey of Jesus Christ coming into our world and returning to the God from whom he came. We have hints of the loneliness of Christ, the loneliness of all great prophets and leaders. Perhaps the best image of the loneliness of this unique Person among us is seen in his journey into the desert. We can read the account in Matthew 4 or Luke 4. "Jesus was led by the Spirit out into the wilderness." He went alone. Someone has written as a bystander:

> I came reverently into the desert place, respecting his time there, his being alone. He was lean, alert, his eyes like glass. If his mother were to see him like this she would be troubled. She would want to take him home, but it cannot be. There is a mysteriousness about his being here, so long fasting, so long alone. Long hours he prayed, eating only the words of the scripture, the declaration of the prophets, and awaiting the gestation of his own teaching. He submitted his life plans to his God and Father, not without tears. Here he struggled about his person, his life, and his mission.
>
> His temptations were the temptations of all humans: the temptation to power, to be saved by the Law, to be satisfied in the flesh. Here he learned by experience what humans desire and how strongly they desire it. The days did not pass easily.
>
> I could feel the ordeal. Satan would love to have him. Why not take the easy way to win the people? Jesus was straining with sweat, straining to be true to who he was and is. He rose and stood up straight and cried out: Begone, Satan. He had found his path. Peace came. He was very still, spent and exhausted but full of peace and truth.
>
> I wanted to go to him as he sank slowly to the sand to rest. I wanted to touch him and say: Holy strong one!
>
> He knows well what it means to be human and how it is sometimes necessary to be lonely and alone. For our sake, he went into the wilderness, led by the Spirit.

Personal images of loneliness

Certain images portray loneliness, without any words. Each person has his or her own. For me, one of these is an empty school in summer. Another one I retain from my childhood on the prairies is the empty farmhouses of people who moved away and did not return. There they stood, silent houses with windows like gaping eyes staring vacantly into space. The paintings of Andrew Wyeth often express loneliness for me, especially *Mrs. Kuerner* sitting alone with her back to me looking out of a bare window, and *Christina* on the hillside looking up at the old farmhouse at the top of the hill. Another painting by Adrian van Rooy portrays an old woman sitting in the dark doorway of a very dilapidated house. Silhouettes have a similar effect for me.

Some images of loneliness are not quite lonely but have a quiet beauty to them: the lone bird against the sky, a solitary sailboat on a wide sea, a single star in a crescent moon, or a lonely planet brilliant in the sky before the darkness reveals the lesser lights, an unaccompanied jogger running along the shore of a quiet lake, a lone horse grazing in a pasture. Most people if asked would not reply that loneliness is in any way beautiful. But is there not something strikingly beautiful about a single rose standing alone in garden or vase, more beautiful than a whole bouquet of roses? Its uniqueness can be seen and appreciated. Our uniqueness, of course, pleases and frightens us.

Clues to the "cure" for loneliness

I would like to present the single rose as a clue to a cure for loneliness: arriving at that moment in life when we can, without fear, know our separateness and uniqueness, find our own centre. That centre is not walled around, nor need we fill the space around it. Rather, we can move in and out of our centre just as we go in and out of our homes, learning compassion for ourselves and for all others who know the loneliness of their own uniqueness as we do. In our centre, silence becomes the warm velvet caressing us. Silence bathes us, refreshing us. Our loneliness becomes a comfortable solitude filled with life.

It is fascinating to watch a young baby. Every baby is alone in a way, spending much time alone. He is too new to be either fully known or fully grown. The baby cannot communicate verbally with others, yet he seems in no way lonely. We are infinitely enriched by his presence, filled with wonder at the newness which was not there some months ago. The baby may offer us another clue to the cure for loneliness: the ongoing, never diminishing interest in and discovery of life.

It is good to learn, or learn again, to be alone. In fact, we are never alone; but that discovery has to be made in solitude. We can learn to go in and out of our house, our centre, from solitude to community and back, in an ebb and flow whose rhythm is like that of the ocean, the rhythm of life itself. Many or most of us are afraid of what we may find at the centre where our true self resides, and so we break rhythm and run away. We are like the lonely little boy in *Elvis and His Secret* who says: "I want to be alone but not feel it."[2] Elvis feels not needed because "the others know plenty of people" and "lonesome people aren't needed." His friend-in-the-making, Peter, says lonesome people are needed even more than the others. His reasoning is: "They are needed because they know more about loneliness" and so will be more caring of others; and it's important "to be careful with people, to take care of each other."

In his book, *The Loneliness Factor*, Rolheiser quotes Karl Rahner as saying: "We do not feel loneliness. We *are* loneliness," and that because we are made to share life and individuality with God.[3] We have an infinite capacity that no human can fill: only God. Rainer Maria Rilke, the German poet, expresses this aching hunger for God in a most wistful poem:

You, neighbour God
(Du, nachbar Gott)

If sometimes in the night
I rouse you with loud knocking, I do so
Only because I seldom hear you breathe

and know you are alone. (Du bist allein in saal.)
And should you need a drink, no one is there
to reach it to you, groping in the dark.
Always I hearken. Give but a small sign
I am quite near.

Between us there is but a narrow wall,
and by sheer chance; for it would take
merely a call from your lips or from mine
to break it down
and that without a sound.

The wall is builded of your images.

They stand before you hiding you like names,
And when the light within me blazes high
that in my inmost soul I know you by,
the radiance is squandered on their frames.

And then my senses, which too soon grow lame
exiled from you, must go their homeless ways.[4]

Does this poem not touch the very core of our loneliness, the loneliness we share? Who indeed is the one "groping in the dark"? Who is the one experiencing the going of "homeless ways"? Rilke's poetry has expressed what prose cannot fathom. And this infinite capacity, which is also our loneliness, is both our glory and our suffering.

Father Rolheiser distinguishes different kinds of loneliness:

- alienation which is unhealthy;
- restlessness which is normal;
- fantasy which can be quite out of touch with reality;
- rootlessness which can unhinge us from our sense of belonging.

Another writer, Martha Lear,[5] speaks of two main kinds of loneliness: the loneliness of emotional isolation (lack of intimacy and attachment) and the loneliness of social isolation (lack of friends and community).

But this book is not aiming to analyze, theorize or even theologize. All of this has been done better by others. As the title indicates, this book is meant to share our loneliness and our stories as well as the helps and "cures" some of us have found for this condition which is not a disease though it is a dis-ease. Loneliness is in fact something with which we may not only become at ease but may actually embrace and turn into a friend.

In sharing people's stories, I try to be faithful to my belief that what we really long for is to be truly known, and, being known, to be loved as we are. For this to happen we may take to heart these words of Robert Frost in *Revelation:*

> We make ourselves a place apart
> Behind light words that tease and flout
> But oh, the agitated heart
> Till someone find us really out.
> ......
> But so with all, from babes that play
> At hide-and-seek, to God afar,
> So all who hide too well away
> Must speak and tell us where they are. (1913)

This is what the Incarnation is about. It is the revelation of self that God has made to us. Did not Jesus say, "I call you friends, because I have made known to you everything I have learned from my Father" (John 15:15).

> Loneliness makes a winter's night
> seem twice as long
> ...So stay awhile,
> we both [all] have stories that are hungry to be told.
> ...The yes and our hello said no to loneliness.
>
> "Loneliness" *(The Best of Paul Williams)*

Being young is not easy

One of the most heart-breaking statistics of our time is the increased incidence of suicide among the young, not only youth but even children. What a lonely death that must be! What a lonely child or youth who would take such measures to disappear before life has been lived! Thoughts of suicide are not stranger to many teenagers in the extremes of emotion in which they live. I, for one, would not like to relive my teen years. Sometimes then I was not so sure it was worth it. Now I know it is.

Alienation among teens

Two memories in particular I record from my teen years: my lonely disillusionment that the fun things always came to an end; my shyness that made me fear not having a good time at whatever event was afoot.

About the first, I was right in that all things are passing; or we pass and have to leave them behind. This fact of life was a strong factor in my vocation and choice of religious life in the Congregation of St. Joseph. I had the conviction that in such a life God would be the centre. My work would be God's and nothing would be lost or wasted. This is, of course, equally true of any dedicated life: married, single or communal. But for me life in community would be something I would never have to give up or leave behind, since heaven would be the communion of saints forever.

As for the second problem, I received help from an older sister of mine. When I went into a doldrum and announced that I was not going to go to the annual community picnic, she questioned me kindly, seeming to sense my loneliness. I told her I wouldn't have a good time anyway so why should I go. My popular sister answered in this vein:

> When you go to a party or dance, or anywhere, don't think about whether you will have a good time or whether people will like you or pay attention to you. Instead, think: How can I give other people a good time or make them feel comfortable? Be the first to say hello. Let others know you are glad to see them. Everybody is wondering, "Will I have a good time?" If everyone waits for the other person to speak first, no one will have a good time. If you give other people a good time, you will find when you come home that you enjoyed yourself and had a good time too. It works.

She was right. But I was not totally cured. So when I went to boarding school some years later and got blamed in a minor misdemeanour, I thought it was the end of the world for me. Now no one would like me. Everyone must be looking at me and shunning me. Thank goodness one of my teachers saw my withdrawal and diagnosed it correctly. She pointed out to me that the principal who had humiliated me had long forgotten about it (I just happened to be the one she got her hands on to make a spectacle of!). And, as for my fellow students, they were on my side! I alone was nursing the hurt. She suggested I test it out. Again, she was right. These two lessons stood me in good stead in my maturing and growth. I was able to take advice and correction without feeling my person was disapproved, defective or destroyed.

In our tests we want desperately to belong and be accepted because we are not yet sure who we are or whether we can stand on our own or whether we are acceptable persons. It is like learning to walk all over again on a different level. "What if, disconnecting from parents and home in order to establish independence, I perish?" our inner self asks.

Loneliness among university students and in homes

Recently an article in the press on cults warned that the loneliness of students in universities makes them prime targets for recruitment. Appealing to their loneliness, the cult offers groupiness and belonging and, especially, "answers" that seem to give security. Young people easily get "hooked" before they realize it—and it may be as hard to get unhooked from a cult as from a drug. Students who have come to study in a new city with nothing familiar and few friends to relate to are vulnerable to a friendly invitation and may be led to disastrous moral and legal entanglements. Youth cannot wait to make real friends, so poignant is the loneliness. Or they fear to trust relationships that they know will be temporary with the academic year.

But it is not only on campuses of universities that youth feel alone. Loneliness and alienation in the home are often behind the exodus of young people to the streets of big cities where they seek their "own kind." The exodus may be less a desire for freedom from controls than a real loneliness they hope to overcome by joining the groovy set in the city, trying drugs that "turn them on" or simply living in a hostel. I often pass by the Under 21 House and its occupants who empty out into Allan Gardens in Toronto. My heart goes out to them, and I am glad there are adults who welcome them off the streets and show concern for their health and well-being. I suppose these youth wonder who this "little old lady" is that passes by and says hello and asks how things are at Under 21. It was my concern for these young people and my deep desire to help them find their meaning in life that prompted me to write them this letter:

To youth, my young brothers, sisters, friends:

Ages passed. Time moved on. Fishes left the water, flew in air or walked on land. Out of nature's ways the miracle of man, the wonder of woman!

Ages more were lived and some recorded, first in memory, then in stone and ink. Families formed—mothers and fathers, grandmothers and grandfathers, great-great-grandparents.

Then one day particularly you were born new into the world. You were held. And you evoked a smile, a smile of tenderness because you were so small. The long, long human story that day became your story. All that formed you is in you now; and yet, none other has ever been or ever will be as you in your perfection.

Deep within your being is a source of life, a spring of water. Drink from your own well and be all that is good and noble, true and best. Seek this stream within you. See your face reflected there. Search into your deep desire. Then go and do what you have seen there and have heard. There is a way to fulfill this vision. And life itself, though you pass through pitfalls, trials, errors, darkness—life itself will see you through to wholeness. And you will leave to those who come seeking and searching the paths of those who went before, a shining moment in the story that will stir them to their own undiscovered depths. They too then will rise and walk and write their lives for all to read. And so the human story will not die but reach its full and glorious ending.[1]

Taking to the streets

A young man I know quite well who had "got into a lot of trouble" complained, "I've had a hard life." Yes, he had. It was no comfort that he had brought it on himself for he said, with tears, "I don't know why I do the things I do." He had gone with the crowd to keep friends. It was he who did the dares, the petty thefts, the shop-lifts. But when he was caught, the "friends" were nowhere to be seen. Not one stood by him. Yet, in order to maintain such friendships, the young man went from petty to serious misconduct. It took him a long, long time, many lonely hours in detention, many pangs of disillusionment, and a faithful young woman who loved him before he finally discovered that the route he had taken was no solution to the loneliness he felt.

We adults, do we not feel sorrow for the inherent loneliness of growing up? Do we not desire to help the passage from teen to adult by staying around and standing by so that the young do not feel entirely disconnected, so that they know there is a warm human hand there if they need it and want to grab for it?

One passes by arcade games centres and notices the lack of communication among the participants. Each is wrapped up in his or her own machine. It always strikes me as the ultimate in loneliness to play alone. Likewise, sitting on a subway train on a quiet Sunday, one sees the youth with their Walkmans and earphones and one wonders. Is it a way of finding much-needed solitude from an otherwise scattered world? Or is it one more symbol of isolation. It looks lonesome. It sometimes seems to say: "You're not there."

Younger children

Much can be written on the loneliness of children, the younger ones. It is not to be confused with the ability and even the need of children to be alone in the world they are both imagining and discovering. As Ralph Waldo Emerson wrote:

Respect the child. Be not too much his parent.
Trespass not on his solitude.

But there is a real loneliness experienced by children who are rejected, abandoned or blamed for what is beyond their understanding or their capacity for coping. We experience in our society the growing phenomenon of broken homes and divided families, and it is difficult to gauge the confusion, fear, insecurity and loneliness that results for children. One set of Canadian statistics indicates that 40%

of our children will find themselves in one-parent homes before the age of 18.² This is not to lay blame on separated or divorced parents who already have enough anguish over broken relationships. Rather it acknowledges the fact of lonely children and invites a concerted and generous response by adult society. Some adults have taken the loneliness of children to heart and have set up helps such as Families In Transition (FIT) and guidelines for coping with separation.

In my travels on many buses, trains and airplanes I have had occasion to meet many lonely children. I have invited them to sit with me since many people seem uncomfortable or simply do not want the bother. Let me share some of these encounters. They are not without their touch of sadness but contain their quantity of charm and resourcefulness as well.

Once en route from New York to Toronto, we were held up at customs. The culprit was a small Jewish boy nine years of age. He was travelling alone with, in the words of the customs' officer, "everything including the kitchen sink" in his various bags.

The boy was questioned at length. "Where are you going? Are you alone? Why are you alone? Is someone going to meet you? What's all this stuff you are carrying?" He answered bravely to every query.

The boy was, of course, the last to board the bus and all impatient eyes were on him. I moved over and invited him to sit beside me. As we drove off I tried to put him at ease by telling him my name and asking his. That started him on his life story—all nine years of it!

He was coming from a Jewish boarding school in New York City. His mother lived in the West, his father in Toronto. He had a big brother somewhere. He was returning to live in Toronto. He asked me:

"Do you ever cry?"

I said, "Yes, sometimes. Sometimes we have to cry when we feel bad. It's all right to cry."

He told me: "I never cry out loud. I just cry to myself. My father always told me whenever I cried, 'I'll give you something to cry about,' and then he'd hit me. So whenever I feel like crying, I go to a closet or someplace where no one will see me. Then no one knows I'm crying.

He kept looking up at me. He had the most beautiful large brown eyes I have ever seen. He told me where he lived and wanted so much for me to know his street. In fact, he seemed almost surprised that I had not heard the name of his street before. I felt his surprise turn to anxiety, as if he feared that the street might no longer be there. I told him I would be sure to look it up on my map when I got to Toronto. He was so happy to know that I also would be living in Toronto.

I asked him if someone was going to meet him at the bus terminal. He said: "My dad." We chatted and then he fell asleep, his curly head nodding against my arm.

When we arrived in Toronto after 11 hours, we got off the bus and the boy looked about for his father. He was not there. He had sent a cab! The boy smiled at me, bit his quivering lip and waved goodbye as the cab-driver ushered him into the car with his bag and baggage.

Another encounter occurred in the West as I passed through the prairies. It was a short encounter. I sat with a young girl who was en route alone to stay with her grandparents.

She told me: "I just came from the hospital. I take convulsions. Mommy says maybe I'll be better with my grandparents. I used to have a sister. She wasn't really my sister but we adopted her. She was pretty. Whenever we got in trouble my daddy always said it was my fault. My sister got killed. I also have asthma."

The little girl took from her purse a school picture of herself, wrote her name on the back and gave it to me. She wanted me to remember her. I do remember her. I remember a very grave child, a suffering child already burdened beyond her understanding.

Heading up to the Yellowhead in a very crowded bus, an overnight ride, I had the company, once again, of a child six years old. Her mother sat ahead with another on her knees. My little companion smiled up at me and whispered: "I have mandarin oranges in this bag for me and my brother. Would you like one?"

"Not right now, thank you."

She told me about school, about her teacher, about her friends in grade one. I asked her the names of her friends that she played with. She enumerated them and singled out some as her "very, very best friend." She was a bright child with an unusually advanced vocabulary.

To entertain her, since she showed no signs of dozing off, I showed her the numerous snapshots, obituary cards and the "holy matter" in my office book.

I had in my book a picture in black and white by Rouault, *Christ Mocked*. It is not a pretty picture. I passed it by. But she noticed that I had missed one and insisted on seeing it. When she held it, she turned to me and said:

"He is a poor man."

"Child," I thought, "you speak truer than you know."

We carried on for a great long time. Suddenly she looked up at me again and said: "Do you know my name? You don't know my name, do you?"

"No, I don't."

Then she pronounced it carefully in a whisper and made me repeat it.

"It's a beautiful name," I said. I had learned from all these children what I already knew myself: how important it is that someone knows our name, knows us. That is our security. She asked me where I was going to get off. I told her Edmonton and she told me: "My daddy lives in Edmonton." I got the picture.

Finally after feeling the imitation fur on my coat and saying she liked to go to sleep with something soft and furry near her face, she fell asleep on the cuffs of my coat sleeves.

En route once more in the vicinity of New York, I sat down in the bus opposite a pretty little girl who was occupying the front seat behind the driver, all by herself. On the platform, a tall man was standing with a blonde woman. I presumed they were the parents.

The child called out the door: "Daddy! Tell the driver my name so he can call me when I'm supposed to get off." He reassured her. Again she called out the door: "Daddy, see you soon, eh?" Anxiety! I could feel it.

The bus driver asked if someone was meeting her when she got off. She and the father both answered. She said, "Yes, my mother."

"So that's it!" I thought. The little girl has two homes. The blonde woman is not her mother. The child ignored the woman and addressed only her father. I seemed to feel her unarticulated resentment.

We moved off with the child standing up and waving to her daddy. This story is repeated many times with variations of name and place.

By their very physical smallness, by their very childhood, they are vulnerable and they are victimized. Not always intentionally or because people are evil, but simply because of painful circumstances and the failures, divisions and separations that adults suffer, the children suffer greatly, though with wonderful resilience.

Of the world's 2 billion children, 70 million now live without families, making their way as best they can (U.N. Statistics).[3]

The late Catherine Doherty writes about "the sobbing of children rejected." She says, "They don't let anyone know about it. But those of us who love them hear their sobbing."[4] As individuals, as church, as society we can hear and sense and receive and assuage the loneliness of children, not by spoiling them (a temptation) but by welcoming them.

It seems to me that the loneliness of children in our time reaches right back to the womb. The late Marshall McLuhan, communication expert, had this to say about it: "The distances we feel between people has carried into the distance between a mother and her unborn child, so great that she cannot relate to her child as a person but only as an 'it'."[5] If we now have *in vitro* fertilization, we will no doubt in the relatively near future achieve *extra utero* gestation (that is, development of the embryo-foetus in a mechanically-produced and artificially-supported environment up to and including birth). What a lonely beginning that would be. No use to say the unborn are not conscious. Everything that has been experienced remains. An amusing little story may be a propos here:

A little boy in his little cot upstairs could not sleep. He called downstairs, "Mommy, come up. I'm scared in the dark."

Mother called back up, "You don't have to be afraid. God is everywhere and God is upstairs with you, dear."

A silence followed. Then the little voice was heard once more calling down, "Mommy, I want somebody with skin on."

We might apply these honest words from conception to adulthood.

Scriptural consolation

Jesus said, "Let the little children come to me" and he laid his hands on them, touched them and embraced them. And he blessed them, too. Let every child and every youth hear those words, "Come to me." Let them hear Jesus, also feeling rejected, saying, "How often have I longed to gather your children, as a hen gathers her brood under her wings, and you refused!" (Luke 13:34). That is how he would enclose the young with his love.

This image of the wings of God enfolding is quite common in scripture. Under the shelter of God's wings we are not to fear (Psalm 36). Even if my father and mother desert me, God will care for me still (Psalm 27:10). "Does a woman forget her baby at the breast or fail to cherish the child of her womb? Yet, even if these forget, I will never forget you" (Isaiah 49:15). Jesus looked with such love on the young man, even though the young man did not follow him because of his riches (Matthew 19:13-15). We are known deeply and completely by the One who always loves us dearly. No one can steal us away from God. How our children and our youth need to know that and hear it again and again. Indeed, have it sung to them as they are rocked to sleep or bid good-night.

> For it was you who created my being,
> knit me together in my mother's womb.
> I thank you for the wonder of my being,

for the wonders of all your creation.

Already you knew my soul,
my body held no secret from you
when I was being fashioned in secret
and molded in the depths of the earth.

Your eyes saw all my actions,
they were all of them written in your book;
every one of my days was decreed
before one of them came into being.
...
See that I follow not the wrong path
and lead me in the path of life eternal.

(Psalm 139)

Lessening loneliness

• Have a pet or a good hobby. This might be music, volunteering regularly as a helper, a sport (that is not aggressive or all-demanding).

• Read good books that will stir your interest and ideals.

• Reach out to other young persons who seem to be alone.

• Join a youth group. If there is none in your parish or area, ask adults to help you start one.

• Find an adult you can trust and talk to when you are lonely.

• Don't let anyone pressure you to do what you do not really want to do. Liquor and drug "friends" will let you down and leave you "hooked" and isolated.

• Don't blame yourself for parents' problems, but don't be too hard on them either. They are also trying to cope. Never forget you are a good person.

• Dream of a better world. You have a particular place in it and your contribution to make early or late in your life.

• Make friends with God. You are never alone. Prayer, in whatever form you like, is a life-line. Great persons have been sustained by their faith in and relationship to God.

• Being you is naturally a little lonely, but you belong to all of us. We are together on this planet. Help to love and care for it.

• If you are an adult, reach out to the young. Love them. But don't smother them. Sense their loneliness and give that extra support.

Alone in my wheelchair

On the subway trains of Toronto there are many advertisements. One caught my eye. It was in four parts. The first frame was a close-up of the face of an attractive young woman smiling out at me. The second frame was taken of her whole body... seated in a wheelchair. The third was taken from some distance. In the fourth, the woman had receded into the background. Or rather, the viewer had moved away, far away from her. The caption read: Please don't walk away from us.

The ad is a study in the loneliness of handicapped persons. The causes of that loneliness are in them but also in the rest of us, in their limitations and our fears, in our limitations and their fears. Were we to see only the face, we would respond differently. When we see frame two, we begin to back away.

Jean Vanier has done perhaps more than any other single person, except the handicapped themselves, to banish the fear and even sometimes near revulsion we have toward those physically impaired or mentally "deficient," and to welcome the handicapped into the active life and social milieu of our society. By inviting us to come and be with and live with handicapped persons, Vanier has helped us to discover first hand that they are not only human but also neither better nor worse than any so-called "normal" person—with perhaps one exception: the mentally handicapped are usually high on affection. We deny ourselves some deep and rewarding relationships when we shy away from people handicapped in some way. Like the boy Peter who reasoned that lonely people are more needed because they understand loneliness best, we could say the handicapped are more practised at it than most of us. They have learned to live with loneliness often better than most. If the mentally handicapped are less articulate about loneliness, this does not mean they feel it less.

But let me, instead of commenting, introduce you to some persons with handicaps whom I have known for a long time and whom I interviewed for this book. They were generous in sharing their stories with me and with you.

Doreen's story

Doreen is somewhat though not severely handicapped with cerebral palsy. I spoke to her about the topic of loneliness because I remembered how when she lived alone in a small apartment she used to suffer quite grievously from loneliness, despite the fact that she went to work every day. At the time, she came to stay with us for some days to assuage the pain of it. Because of her muscular impairment, it took her a very long time to rise and prepare herself to go out as well as to get to work. The effort left her exhausted. At that time also, Doreen used to practically devour her friends, so glad was she to have them around. She laughs about it now and sees that it was an expression of her need rather than of her love.

When I visited Doreen at her home, where she now lives and from which she still goes out to work, I had not seen her for several years. I found a much-changed person. She brought me into her room. I had prepared some questions to help focus on those years of loneliness. Doreen sat before me, composed, self-possessed, well-dressed, with an air of stillness about her, ready to share with me, so that I might share with you, her journey from then to now.

I asked, "Why did you move out to your own apartment in the first place?"

"Because I was advised to learn to manage for myself if I was ever to become an adult. I had to find new avenues. I had to prove I could live on my own. I had to prove to myself and to my family who always thought I was retarded and dependent, 'I'm not on that label'."

She had proved it. But what about the loneliness? I asked her if it was because she had no time to socialize because it took her so long to do everything.

"It wasn't that!" she answered, "It was just that I couldn't bear to be alone because I had no self-worth. I wanted everyone to love me so I'd be worth something. And yet I thought, 'I can't be loved until I'm beautiful, until I'm educated, until I'm slim.' I wanted to be with people who made be feel O.K. I was living through other people, trying to fill up the void. And it doesn't work."

I asked her how she coped with her loneliness? She replied:

"I'd go drinking with a group. But I hated it because they were just trying to cover their anxiety too. I tried emotional religion—wanting to be with sisters who cared about me, wanting hugs at church. Or I'd want to see T.G. my favourite priest to get a big hug from him. But then they were all sent away—one to Prince Rupert, another to Boston, you to New York, and there I was: let down again!

"Another thing I did because of loneliness was I slept a lot, like from Friday night to Sunday noon. What a waste of life that was! I also watched hours and hours and hours of TV—anything to try to fill the void.

"And I fantasized a lot.

"I joined a prayer group for the fellowship. But when I wasn't healed of my handicap, they sort of accused me.

And when I didn't speak in tongues or prophesy, they sort of told me I wasn't doing it right. Sometimes I'd fall asleep at the prayer and they said that was wrong. Finally I just gave up.

"I cried and cried. I tell you I cried for months right here in this room—I had moved back home by then."

What helped her most to get out of the loneliness she felt? I put the question to her and she answered:

"Well, I just put myself behind me, you might say. Loneliness is self-centred, that's what it is. So when everything else was gone, I turned to God. I said, 'God, here's your chance to show your stuff.' I just unloaded my burden on God and God took it.

"I thought: God loves those people who hurt me too. People are there when it's fine with you, but when you're in trouble they don't want to be there. But God is always there—every minute, every circumstance. I made a choice to believe that. I put God first in my life. You see, there is a void in us that no one can fill. Only God can fill it.

"God is not a feeling. God is reality.

"I thought to myself, 'Doreen, do you love God because of what God gives you or because God is God and God is good?' That's not fantasy. I don't fantasize any more. I live in reality. That is a solid foundation of truth.

"So I accepted myself. And God sent certain people like H. who called me up every day. He talked many hours on the phone and said: 'Doreen, will you please promise me one thing? Will you please love yourself?' He moved away but he had done his job with me."

At this point the phone rang. Doreen picked it up and with a smile, as if the person were standing there in the room before her, she welcomed the caller. It was obvious to me that it was someone who needed her ear and trusted her. She spoke for a few moments after listening, then kindly asked the person if she might call back since she had a visitor in the room. She replaced the receiver and looking

back up at me from her easy chair she looked like a queen surveying the domain of her comfortably furnished room, pretty in her red silk dress that fell gracefully in soft folds. Then she took up where she had left off:

"Now I don't worry what people think. I don't do things to make people love me. I don't do things on a committee to feel I'm doing something, to cover the lonely."

(I confess, I cringed a little at that one. "Do I?" I asked myself in the moment that passed. How many of us do that?)

"You have to face the roar. You can't run from it. I accept the facts. Then I *choose*. I have a choice. I can choose happiness. I can choose how to dress, how to develop myself. I live within myself, with God as my centre. I don't live through other people for my value.

"I'm still learning—like I spent too much money on good clothes and got into debt but now I know why I did that—like eating or drinking or grouping—spending is trying to fill a need. I won't need to do that again. My friend L. helped me by taking my Visa card, with my consent, until I got my bills paid. L. and B. are such good friends. They didn't yell at me for doing what I did. A person knows when they've made a booboo. They don't need someone to yell at them."

Doreen then got up in her somewhat difficult way and proceeded over to the clothes closet, taking out her purchases to show me. They were beautiful, in excellent taste and obviously not cheap. She also related how disgusted and upset her mother, who had accompanied her, had become at this extravagant purchase on a limited budget. But Doreen was not deterred, simply because she was making a choice and was prepared to take the consequences both good and bad. She was not about to be intimidated.

"I stand on my own now. And I stand tall. My good friends took me to the Exhibition and got a wheelchair and drove me so I didn't get exhausted. We had a ball. They are real friends, but I don't depend on them for my self-value. I'd like to marry but not because of my need. If the right person comes it will be good, but it must be mutual love and respect: 'I have weaknesses, you have weaknesses. I have strengths, you have strengths. My strength can help your weakness, your strength can help my weakness. We are helpmates.'"

I thought I was indeed hearing wisdom from this woman who had been through so much both exteriorly and interiorly, who had hopes and desires but no fantasies. She finished off with:

"I find now people tell me about their pain and I can understand. I can say I know what that feels like. I can share my life and it helps them. Like when I went to Heritage, we sat in the lobby and talked about our lives. It was great.

"And I tell them how I got over being lonely by putting myself behind myself. I tell them how I stand on my own value and how God is right there all the time."

I was truly edified by this woman who had grown light years in ten. Everything about her bespoke one who knows, one who has accepted her life. Through the loneliness of broken fantasies, putdowns from impatient people at work, and the sheer difficulties of survival and operation, her handicap has become her friend, part of who she is, the person she has befriended. It was not without many false starts, much painful disappointment and abundant tears that she arrived at this maturity and peace. Her Bible too has become a faithful friend through which her strength is renewed like the eagle's (Psalm 103:5). She reads it with faith and confidence, spending extended time in quiet meditation on Saturday mornings. I know Doreen will continue to be a strength, in turn, to many who are suffering the pangs of loneliness because of their handicap. That is why I came home to my typewriter and wrote her story.

Charles' story

In writing this chapter on the loneliness of the handicapped, I cannot fail to write of Charles, a longtime friend who has enriched my life immeasurably. He is a quadriplegic. He was involved in an auto accident in 1961. He has been in hospital ever since; but do not think that he has been vegetating.

I first met Charles when one of our sisters was a patient in the sanatorium in Weston. Charles was in the Extendicare of an adjoining building. One day when I went to visit Sister Maria Consolata, she said to me:

"There's a young man here that I want you to meet. I think you will like each other. He is a poet. I told him about you so why don't you go and see him."

I did. It was instant friendship. The friendship has remained, though I blush at how seldom I visit him. Every time I do, I wonder why I deprive myself so long. He always cheers me up.

Charles is still out in Weston, in the new wing called Westpark Hospital. He has a motorized chair now which allows him much more mobility. With the help of friends and Wheel-Trans he has taken classes in the city. He has exhibited paintings, published and read poetry and won awards in both.

It was not always so. The days, the months and even years following the highway accident on a wet August day in 1961, in which his neck was broken, were heavy with loneliness, almost despair, for Charles. Though born in Toronto, he had moved with his family to Texas when still a child. When he returned to work in Toronto after a hard-living, exciting career as a cowboy, he had neither family nor a large number of people who could support him when he was stricken. Besides, when one is out of circulation, as anyone will know who has had a long illness, people go on with their lives and unintentionally "shelve" the absentee. In addition, Charles's friends found "they couldn't handle it." But he had to handle it.

Five years after the accident, Charles began to write—thoughts that turned to poetry. He found that he could put himself in the place of other people, sense their suffering, know their feelings, share the humanity common to us all. In one of these poems, he writes of the very depth of loneliness, not his own but someone else's:

> He wanted to love
> but feared its power
> he wanted to cry
> but was unable
> to show tears
> he wanted to die
> and hoped for someone
> to change his mind.
>
> One night
> unable to love
> unable to cry
> he chose what was left
> and left no note

as an explanation
Why!

He had indeed plumbed human loneliness. But he also reached the place within which the true self resides indestructible. He quotes Milton:

> The mind is its own place, and in itself
> Can make a heaven of hell,
> A hell of heaven....
>
> *(Paradise Lost)*

Charles began to work on "Paradise Regained." He read, listened to music, followed the city and the world on TV News (if you want to know what is going on, ask him!). He is a man in touch with head, heart and humour. He has learned to live day by day, to see, hear and feel each day, not wait for some medical breakthrough to restore the past. Living day by day, he has turned the days into beautiful years, productive years, years of outreach, of creativity and growth. It takes him a long time to do one of his exquisite pen sketches, but he has lots of time.

In all this process of coping and living, Charles has turned his acute loneliness into true solitude, full of meaning. A short poem by Charles printed on the Westpark Christmas card for 1987 expresses it:

> Snow, with night had fallen.
> Pines cloaked in white stood tall.
> Stillness was alive
> as the owl in flight,
> feathered white,
> slipped quickly
> in and out of sight.

Despite the setbacks he still suffers, such as infections that lay him low for days at a time, this man is alive and will live until he dies. Charles had all the conditions and all the excuses for loneliness. They say the best way out of loneliness is through it. That is the route Charles took. Because he went all the way through, and also because he has written, many others are less lonely. I sometimes think that, had he not been immobilized, he and we might never have discovered how creative he is.

The last time I went to see Charles, I could not find him. No one seemed to know where he was. I waited about an hour, paging and searching. As I was about to leave, he came in surrounded by young students and quite a bit of noise. They had gone to another building to wrap his Christmas presents for him. I scolded him for "taking off like that," and then we had a lovely lunch together.

Mary Lou's story

Let me tell you of a young woman who has known loneliness in its farthest corners, kept an account of it and, daring to look it in the face, has overcome it at every step of the difficult way. Her name is Mary Lou. I first met Mary Lou as a student in residence at St. Joseph's College in 1976 when I was acting dean there. For the writing of this chapter, she has shared her diaries with me. This remarkable woman is a very ordinary person who has kept an extraordinary diary, one which I would like one day to edit and publish. It has the quality of an Anne Frank or an Etty Hillesum.

Mary Lou was a very bright and active young person who excelled in math, wrote poetry, and ran for office in the Ontario Catholic Student Federation and won! Even in those days in London, she kept an account of her thoughts and feelings—and of her loneliness.

"What are your aims for this year, 1973?

"A year of growth, spiritual, emotional, intellectual and to do this I must go out to more people and experience new things. Or perhaps the trick is to experience my everyday activities, to put my whole self into them.

> "By 1974 I'll be 16, in Grade 12.
> "With spring, there comes to me
> A fear
> A fear that I won't be able to respond to spring
> And all its happenings.

Fear that I will be alone.
Fear that I won't be able to follow
those paths I want.
Don't be afraid.
You will never be alone. Jesus Christ
is always with me
And in his light I can follow the paths to discovery.
O Mary Lou, get out and enjoy spring."

(6/3/73)

She senses that her ideas are not always accepted by the other students she desires to serve and represent. She worries about not hearing from Mark. She wants to have good relationships. She philosophizes.

"I am so lonely, so lonely, dear God. Teach me to love. I guess loving people can be lonely.

"Grant that I may work hard and wisely. Please, Mark, write soon, oh God, soon.

"What my life needs is a lot more discipline [...] in that I plan ahead. Not that I live for the future, because each day should be lived with fullest enthusiasm.

"I know that there is no single rule or key to a good life. Life is a continual education."

(5/11/73)

If there is one thing this girl does not lack it is enthusiasm for life. Her diaries are marked by it. They are peppered with "I will try" and zest for continual growth, discovery and determination.

Still, in the midst of this enthusiasm are the deep surges of loneliness:

"So often I feel unsure. I haven't received love from where I have given it. I feel as if what I have to give is rejected. But probably I haven't given enough, haven't loved enough. Every other person is as afraid to give as I, as fearful of being rejected as I.

...the person that is me has many sides.

> Some you have never met.
> I would gladly introduce you
> If I didn't think you couldn't care less." (7/7/74)

The family moved to Toronto. The move was painful, the experience of loneliness poignant:

> "I want a friend, Lord,
> I want a friend to talk to and do things with and laugh with. Lord, hear my prayer.

> "I would tell you of loneliness
> Of the hot smothering tears that make me sick [...]
> Of pain that doctors can't cure
> Of eating cheese and crackers alone
> Watching an Elvis Presley movie on Saturday night
> Of going to Mass alone
> Coming home alone
> And talking to no one [...]
> Of facts and prayers." (25/9/74)

Later, as she meets new friends and receives letters from friends in London:

> "Of rediscovering joy at the piano [...]

> Of not being afraid to say who I was
> Of saying I will be your friend. And I was.

> "And lastly I will tell you
> of friendship I have known
> Of love so deep, so real that it couldn't be labelled
> Of seeing your face and being filled with joy
> Of being hurt so deeply and you came to me [...]
> Of seeing the walls between us
> Of seeing those strange walls fall down
> Of the happiness I felt then
> I would tell you of myself."

This girl, who writes with a ruthless honesty and speaks with a disarming truthfulness, addresses God as you would address one very near. At one point she writes:

> "Do you mind if I take a temporary leave of absence, Lord, from talking to you in the traditional sense? Then,

perhaps if I approach you on a different level, or stand back a little—quite a little—I will see a more real truth. [...] Do you mind if I don't always capitalize 'you' since I'm talking to you as a friend?"

Then on November 20, 1974, during an Antioch Retreat with her school companions, Mary Lou was stricken with a brain hemorrhage. This young woman, so enthusiastic for life and so eager and ready to work on it, was cut down. She was comatose for nearly seven weeks and spent the next eight months returning to a functional state after brain surgery. It was a long, long way back. It was a lonely way back. There is, of course, a gap in her diaries. When she returns to her writing she notes:

"I can't really remember too much about it. Just things as told me by my peers and my family. I can't remember that far back in my memory, which is probably just as well."

She begins a monumental and relentless struggle to regain and sustain her active life and interests and especially her relationships which she feels have been shattered:

"Please help me in my awful state of affairs, with my friends and with my enemies, and with everyone I know and can love [...] I'M GETTING BETTER until I am at my old stronghold before I was ill."

It is a day-to-day struggle. Still the determination never flags and at times a saving humour flashes out:

"Lord, I would want so much to be up there with you

Right now.

Why was I not taken on having my brain hemraage? hemorhage? Because I can't spell it! Right?"

Mary Lou experienced a problem of communication. She spoke rapidly and in a sort of monotone and was often asked to repeat. It was frustrating as well as humiliating:

"I must conquer my own inhibitions about talking to people, to get rid of this awful fast talking. Speak louder,

Mary Lou. But it doesn't really end there, Mary Lou, it continues for many a long day and night."

She makes an assessment of her talents:

"It's very weird to realize that talents you used to have are no longer there at all.

Talents like writing a good short story in French or English.

Talents like getting an answer right in math class.

That too is gone.

Talents like saying the right thing at the right time is gone or almost gone (but perhaps it will come back slowly).

Talents like being sure about words and not having to go over them again.

Like knowing what must be done and then doing it."

One can feel the very painful limitation this young woman is experiencing. Still she names her present talents:

"What are your talents right now?

"1) Being friendly to people who need a friend, people like me who really need a friend a lot because if I don't I get depressed, and people like C. who is so lonely. Dear Lord, please give her someone to go out with, please, oh please. [The reader of the diaries is constantly astonished at these bursts of concern for others that flash out from this indomitable spirit in the midst of her own struggle.]

"2) Being very kind to people who need kindness like all of the above mentioned.

"For all these I want there to be a *very big prayer* from way, way inside me."

From time to time, Mary Lou wonders:

"I wonder when will I have my ideas back again? When?

"I really do wonder what I would have been like if I had not had my brain hemorrhage. I would have been a completely different person.

"I am not all perfect. I have an injury to my brain. I am not always capable of doing all of the things I would like to do—the same would be true, even if I had not had the brain hemorrhage—always remember that—*please*.

"I wish I had more time to type out my thoughts. I wish I had thoughts to type out. I wish for too much. I am a fool. But still I wish for things. My thoughts should not be on things that I cannot have. *Can not have. Oh God, that hurts!* My thoughts should be on things that I can have [...] please, Lord, let that be a greater number in my life." (26/1/87)

How often she prays for help on her way back to "normalness." How she longs to be normal! Still she always returns to reality, one of Mary Lou's very strong points.

"But I did have a brain hemorrhage. Many things I have lost but many I have found also.

"How do I see myself? As a *developing* person.

"Plan out your life so that it will change in only the way that the *Good Lord* wants it to change. This means *prayer*. " (8/5/87)

"Keep on talking to our Lord, Jesus Christ, and see what answers you get and, boy, do I ever mean it. Because now it is going to be harder for you... an awful lot harder for you, yes, an awful lot harder for you.

"I can continue to grow. Continue on." (6/12/73)

Aware of the many choices closed to her, this young woman nevertheless went on to work with handicapped children, took a typing course, tried a year at university, worked on a political campaign, made a Vanier retreat and moved out of her family home into a community. About the last choice she made careful consideration, listing the positives and negatives. She concluded:

"If I move back home that is O.K. The moving out will be the most important factor... I will have begun a journey that will continue forever. I must stop to think before making any decision (but in an energetic, adventurous spirit and initiative)."

How well Mary Lou describes herself there!

In 1984, Mary Lou met her future husband. She had wondered if it would ever be possible, much as she ardently desired it. She often addressed this hope to her diary and to God. The entries over the following months are a developing story of love, happiness, anxiety about whether the relationship and possibilities were real. She examines her motives. She prays fervently for Dave. She gives thanks over and over for having met him. She appreciates him as a "learning man and a teaching man" who also appreciates her questioning. He is "imaginative, a retrospective, analytical thinker." She recognizes a major difference in their attitude to life:

"He thinks that if you are not a successful person in life, then your life has been a waste. I think that if you put a good effort forward, then your life is a success."

After weighing and praying ("Please help Dave and I to come together in a marriage, oh please!"), Mary Lou finally comes to the decision:

"Today I have realized how much I love David Hunter Marc [...] He is the one in all of this world that I love. I will love him until I die. [...] We have problems. We are not perfect. But together we make a good couple. [...] It will be a hard route to follow in marrying him, a very hard route. But now I want to marry this man."

And marry Dave Hunter Marc she did. The problems were not only hers, for Dave has multiple sclerosis. As the disease has progressed the "route" has become harder indeed. Very much harder. Still she writes that she is glad she made that decision.

It is not only her diaries that are filled with prayer, concern, reality, simplicity, enthusiasm, faith, hope undauntable, thoughtfulness for those less fortunate than herself and boundless gratitude. It is her life that is filled with these, and especially with love, love reaching out of her loneliness, heroic love. This woman of vitality who loves God so much that she even dares to swear at him, who prays not to be "nice, nice" or "that handicapped girl who is very good looking" (which she is), knows that she is part of "your good, lunatic, absurd, upset, disturbing *gigantic* plan. But I still have to ask why? I will be asking that question until I die." All the while she asks the question, Mary Lou keeps living her life to the fullest.

I returned Mary Lou's diaries to her in her apartment. She was there to greet me. We had arranged that while she was out at work, I would talk with that special person who had become her husband: Dave the English student, poet, musician of the electric bass who had played in such groups as Incubus, Cathedral and Madhouse, and now victim of multiple sclerosis.

I asked Dave: "What is your image of loneliness?" His reply was: "Standing on a stage with my electric bass and nobody in the audience." That is the way it is for Dave now. The MS worsens progressively. He is no longer ambulatory. His speech is slow and careful, though quite clear. The audience is not there. The sound is turned off. The fast life is slowed.

But it is not slowed to a halt. The spirit of this man has never died. An English major, he is now close to completing his master's degree. He is full of humour and anecdotes. He said: "I got my MS *honoris causa* before my MA, which will come with a 45-page essay and hard work." Jokingly again, he quoted his now favourite ditty by William Morris which he said describes his situation:

> Christopher Columbus set off not knowing
> where he was going.
> He didn't know where he was when he got there.
> And he did it all on borrowed money.

But on the more serious side, he quoted lines from T. S. Eliot's *Prelude IV*:

> His soul is stretched tight across the skies
> That fade behind a city block

> Of (street) trampled by insistent feet
> At four and five and six o'clock...
> I am moved by fancies that are curled
> Around these images, and cling.
> The notion of some infinitely gentle
> Infinitely suffering thing.
> Wipe your hand across your mouth and laugh;
> The worlds revolve like ancient women
> Gathering fuel in vacant lots.

"It often feels like that: 'gathering fuel from vacant lots.'"

The greatest loss, he says, is mobility, "for which I grieve." Having come out of a society of musicians and university life, he says:

"I find myself trapped. I'm like Dr. Manette in Dickens' *A Tale of Two Cities*. Reduced to being a cobbler, long imprisoned, when asked his name he only knew to reply: '106 North Tower.' That's how it seems to me sometimes up here in the apartment."

I noticed a framed reproduction of Albrecht Durer's *Praying Hands* on the dresser. Dave said these remind him to say the serenity prayer of Alcoholics Anonymous which he finds so helpful:

> God grant me
> the serenity to accept the things I cannot change,
> the courage to change the things I can,
> and the wisdom to know the difference.

Some of the things he has been able to change are as simple as getting a key guard on his typewriter to avoid the frustration of hitting wrong keys because of a lack of precise muscular control.

In the midst of the blow of the diagnosis of MS in the early eighties came the loss of his first wife and the death of a friend and fellow musician, Buzz Sherman, in a motorcycle accident. The family problems of his only brother brought the two of them closer together:

"I started then thinking more about other people, trying to feel their hurting and to help them through, to ease the pain by just being understanding."

Dave has a fund of wonderful memories: being taught by Irving Layton, having travelled across Canada playing guitar and doing sound mix, being steeped in literature and philosophy. He is not culturally poor. Having an artistic nature, he can make treasures of small happenings. At a recent release of Layton's last book, the author recognized Dave and left a kiss on the right hand that had played the electric bass and was now disabled. I teased, "I suppose you haven't washed the hand since?" (He was wearing fingerless leather gloves to protect his hands.)

Together with his wonderful humour and anecdotal bent, Dave has a rich, active and resourceful mind with which he is able to fill the hours he must spend in the apartment, often alone. Still going to class with the aid of Mary Lou, still interested in everything, he bravely battles his limitations. Dave is real. That is the saving quality in the silences between the performances, between "the smell of the grease paint and the roar of the crowd," silences that perhaps prepared him for the time to come, prepared him for the living with loneliness.

Real

> I lie in the darkness
> Of my blackened abode
> As time weaves along
> Her endless road
> And I think of the things
> That I always have done
> And ponder the reason
> Why I'll never be someone
> Real.
>
> I reach with my hand
> For something to feel
> I search with my eyes
> But the darkness conceals

Any image or thing
Any object or mass
I could hold in my grasp
And claim that I held something
Real.

And as I lie here
In my silent room
The blackness enfolds me
Like death in a tomb
And the walls round about
Are but lost to my vision
Yet these thoughts I am thinking
Are tangible, existing
And I know
Yes I know
I am real.

Canadian heroes and heroines

In Canada we have had our several handicapped heroes and heroines: Sondra Diamond, Terry Fox, Steve Fonyo, Rick Hansen, the Famous People Players Theatre under the direction of Diane Dupuy, our handicapped Olympic athletes, and numerous less well-knowns who have, against great odds, reached out of their loneliness. By their example, they invite us all to reach out of ours, to become part of the human race. One line in the movie *The Elephant Man* has stayed with me. It is spoken by the Elephant Man as he turns and faces his pursuers: "I'm human too." The friend with whom I saw the movie remarked as we left the theatre, "That is every one of us."

Scriptural consolation

In the Book of Genesis (32:23ff.), we read the story of Jacob returning from his long exile. He sends his family, possessions and retinue across the river and stays behind to be alone. That night he struggles with God and is left with an injured hip socket. He limps for the rest of his life but he is blest by God with whom he has fought. He is given a new name and he is chosen by God. We are Jacob, scarred, wounded, chosen for life.

In the New Testament, Mark (2:1-12) describes the paralytic carried by his friends and brought to Jesus, at some inconvenience, through the roof. Jesus relieved him of guilt and, in addition, told him to take up his bed and walk. The man made the choice and got up. Like us, especially like those handicapped, the man had to accept the help of friends or family to go where he could not go alone. But it was he who obeyed the call to life, got up, and shouldered his burden. There is more than one way of "getting up" and of shouldering our burden. Often those who must do it without the use of limbs or super-intelligence and who need our help, outstrip us in the spirit of living. They leave their loneliness behind, come out of hiding and live.

Lessening loneliness

• You can make choices within limits. In this you are like every other human being.

• Like everyone else, you have gifts to develop. Discover them and develop them while being realistic.

• Take advantage of whatever services are available to handicapped persons (government, etc.). Reach out in your own way.

• Time is not everything. If it takes you longer to do something, do it anyway.

• You may well be an inspiration to other people. Often our handicaps do not show on the outside but they are there. For your own inspiration, remember Helen Keller whose chances for being lonely were enormous. She broke out of all the obstacles to a full life, a life that has not been forgotten.

• Often physically handicapped persons, as well as mentally handicapped, have qualities of personality that many others do not have, especially in warm relationships. Being totally independent is not the highest goal: no one is! Your need may give other people a happy opportunity to get to know you and to be of service.

• People are often "nervous" around handicapped persons. Set them at ease by simply saying what your need is.

• You can show understanding and the ability to listen to others who need an ear and a listening heart.

• If it feels to you "not fair" that you are handicapped, accept that life isn't fair! It's a gift and a challenge!

• Who you are, your person, is your real value. What you do is good, but what you are is God's creation.

The loneliness of the long-distance runner

This title of the novel by Alan Sillitoe which made a touching motion picture is a fitting title for this chapter on the loneliness of the artist, the one who runs ahead of us proclaiming where we are, interpreting our surroundings and pushing on to the future—alone.

I recently read the autobiography of Rudolph Nureyev, the Russian ballet dancer. What genius! What loneliness! From early childhood he began to tread the lonely path of desire, discipline and difference that led him to become the greatest dancer of his age. Through the decision to defect to the West to pursue his career, through the months and years of being a "foreigner" as well as a celebrity, to his late performance of the Prince in *The Sleeping Beauty*, dominating the stage by his presence and his white costume, Nureyev is an elegant picture of loneliness. At the core of our loneliness is our uniqueness and there is a special uniqueness about a great artist.

Seeing what's unique, new... prophetic rebel

The loneliness of the artist's uniqueness is increased by the hours and hours of working alone (of what I call "garret time"), that must accompany such a one, whether it is the dancer, painter, writer, poet, musician or skater. A niece of mine, a figure skater, comes to mind. Very, very early in the morning, her lone figure could be seen making its way to the rink to practise for several hours before joining her fellow students at school. I think also of Toller Cranston who lived near my house in Toronto. His fame as a world champion figure skater enclosed him. On those occasions when he himself walked his two beautiful dogs, a dalmatian and a hound, people passed him by with a certain awe! He was recently heard to remark that he never skates for pleasure. It is his life's task to skate.

Another factor in the loneliness of the artist is that he or she sees something different, creates something new. Creativity carries with it both a great joy and a certain guilt. If this sounds strange, it may be shown in such questions as the following which the artist asks:

> Is this too great a criticism of what is? Is it setting myself up as the judge of reality and inviting others to accept my judgment? And if they do not, shall I insist? Am I being arrogant? Is my creation a criticism or, worse, an affront, to the work of the Creator, God? Is this loneliness really "hubris"?[1]

Actually, the true artist is the humble artist, but these are the questions implicit in creating. Rollo May, psychologist, writes in *The Courage To Create*:

> Creativity carries an inexplicable guilt. So many artists and poets commit suicide and often at the very height of their achievement. [...] Creativity is a yearning for immortality. It is related to the problem of death. We must die, yet we must struggle against death. Out of the rebellion the creative act is born.[2]

Perhaps it is also out of the rebellion that the guilt comes. The artist, perhaps especially the writer, may have the additional "guilt" of not producing, in the sense of serving, or of not "doing anything" out there, at least not anything thought to be an essential service. The writer may feel this guilt despite the fact that he or she cannot not write. Deep within, we know that without new vision and insight, we are dead. The song "Thank You For the Music" says it:

> Without a song and a dance what are we?
> So I say, "Thank you for the music,
> For giving it to me."
>
> (ABBA)

The prospect of being misunderstood always awaits the artist. He is like the prophet or seer, often drawing responses like: "Take your words [your piece] and go away from here. Do not disturb us in our familiar ways. Who are you to teach us!" It is lonely, putting one's vision out there, giving it form and substance and being, to be judged, received or rejected. The Dutch artist, Vincent van Gogh, wrote words to this effect:

> There may be a great fire in our soul, yet no one ever comes to warm himself at it, and the passers-by only see a wisp of smoke coming through the chimney, and go along their way. Look here, now what must be done? Must one tend the inner fire, have salt in oneself, wait patiently yet with how much impatience for the hour when somebody will come and sit down—maybe to stay? Let him who believes in God wait for the hour that will come sooner or later.[3]

Decades later, a van Gogh painting, *Irises*, sold for $52 million (Cdn) though the artist himself never sold a painting and was hard put merely to survive. That is loneliness. It is a loneliness poignantly expressed in the song "Starry, Starry Night," whose title is based on another of the artist's now famous paintings:

> Starry, starry night, flaming flowers
> that brightly blaze,

Swirling clouds in violet haze...
Colours changing hue,
morning fields of amber green,
Weathered faces lined with pain
Are soothed beneath the artist's loving hand.
And now I understand
What you tried to say to me,
How you suffered for your sanity,
How you tried to set them free.
They would not listen, they did not know how.
Perhaps they'll listen now.
.....
They could not listen, they're not listening still.
Perhaps they never will.

Rollo May says that "genius and psychosis are close together."[4] Is the eccentricity of an elderly Emily Carr or of a Glen Gould, the seclusion of a Salinger or a Solzhenitsyn, the psychosis of a Vincent van Gogh, an Ezra Pound or a Schumann so much to be wondered at? Is it just that we poor mortal ordinary folk cannot comprehend the nature of genius and of true art?

The artist of whatever kind who would conform the work to public opinion in order to succeed is not a true artist since he or she is not making something new but merely repeating the already known and approved. I saw a striking example of this: one artist true but lonely, the other counterfeit yet affirmed.

Emmanuel was asked to do a wall hanging of the *Last Supper*. She designed and produced a cloth piece. There was something fierce in it, nothing like our customary sentimental *Last Supper*'s. This was, after all, a fierce occasion of a body being given and blood being shed. The work was hung in the dining room. It was unacceptable. Another, an inferior "artist," was asked to do a hanging to replace the first one. The new piece was "made to order," pastel, nice, and a little insipid but in-offensive. The lesser artist received praise, the greater received unspoken disapproval and the removal of her art. That is loneliness.

On a grander scale is the story of Emily Carr, one of Canada's painters. She was Canadian-born of British parents. She was never at home in the drawing room or with Victorian art. Nor was she expected to do well as an artist: she was a woman and her subject was not appropriate—native Indian art in its rugged background. As she herself said: "No school taught art big enough."

The tools for her vision were not to be found in her art studies in Victorian England, but among the Post-Impressionists of Paris. At last she was able to paint the large and brilliant strokes of the Haida. She went to the Queen Charlotte Islands, braving the waters and winds around the Misty Isles with her two Indian guides. But when she did succeed in reproducing on canvas the truly magnificent remnants of a great but dying culture, Emily Carr's art was not accepted. Only after Lawren Harris and the others of the Group of Seven recognized her genius did the public respond. Did Harris realize that Klee Wyck, "the laughing one," so named by the Indian people, was to be an historian as well as an artist? She studied what she painted. She loved it. She made a record in words and in art of the wonderful artistic and spiritual culture of the Haida and the Nootka which can never be replaced. She wrote:

> The object of my work is to get the totem poles in their own settings. The Indians do not make them now and they will soon be a thing of the past. I consider them real art treasures of a passing race.[5]

There was indeed something quite selfless about Emily Carr's art. Fortunately, the Haida have begun to reconstruct their spiritual heritage and its expression in the carven poles. Undoubtedly, Emily Carr contributed to the continuation of this art by capturing the real objects on canvas and bringing them to the galleries where they would stir us to appreciation.

Carr was faithful to her vision and to her art. But it was a lonely road. The CBC made a film about her and entitled it, *Little Old Lady on the Edge of Nowhere*. In her late years, she found companionship with her dogs and a monkey. That is loneliness.

Writers as artists

Turning now to the writers as artists, we might call this section: "Far from the Madding Crowd."[6] It is of the nature not only of writing, but of the writer, to seek seclusion and solitude. Not that writers are separate from humanity, for they read humanity very well and experience it in themselves deeply. But the loneliness, physical and intellectual, is both price and reward for their fidelity to interpreting and describing the human story. Numerous distinguished writers have taken up residence in the backwoods of New England, following the tradition of Thoreau including: Robert Penn Warren, John Updike, Norman Mailer, Alexander Solzhenitsyn, Kurt Vonnegut, John Kenneth Galbraith, and, perhaps most notably, J. D. Salinger of *Catcher in the Rye* fame. Salinger was interviewed by stealth, as it were, by a journalist who quotes him as saying:

In ways I regret ever having been published; it's the insanest profession. If you're lonely, as most writers are, write your way out of it![7]

In some sense, this is excellent advice for anybody. By writing, we experience what Aristotle called a "catharsis" or cleansing of the mind and emotions. We also get in touch with our unconscious and bring it to light. There we also touch what is universal to all humankind and become connected to all.

Speaking of this connectedness and of what is universal, one must confront Jean-Paul Sartre, the late French writer and philosopher. Sartre, more than anyone else in the literary field, carried the loneliness of the writer to the ultimate extreme, fashioning it into a philosophy of being called "radical existentialism." In so doing, he practically lost touch with what all of us have in common, namely, humanness. He also lost touch with God and with joy—though he had humour. Sartre was so determined to figure it all out rationally that he had to get rid of the Holy Ghost once and for all, as he himself said. He never took the leap of faith of his predecessors, Descartes and Kierkegaard, a faith by which suffering, albeit mysterious, has some meaning.

I do not condemn Sartre. It seems evident that adverse circumstances which dehumanize, in his case the disruption and absurdity of a world war, not only cast doubt on all formerly held principles but even construct the very experience of ultimate loneliness: being left alone, on your own, in a world of meaningless suffering, without community and without God (as it seems).

> After World War II, with the human condition more precarious than ever, with humanity facing the mushroom-shaped ultimate absurdity, existentialism and our time came together in Jean-Paul Sartre.[8]

With Sartre, the word "alienation" became commonplace. Sartre concluded that the only way to attain meaning was to forge oneself into a human by choices. The "other," who stands in the way, becomes the enemy in such a view.

Existentialism, which denies that common "essence" of being human possessed by every person from the beginning of existence, has been called a "mood" of philosophy rather than a system. Indeed, Sartre was primarily an artist, rather than a philosopher. He propagated his ideas and expressed the condition of the age, in Europe and North America at least, by means of his art as a writer. He portrayed the disillusionment and "the spiritual vacuum of the century" in novels and plays: *No Exit*, *Les Mots*, *Nausea*, *The Condemned of Altona*.[9] His works of literary art had a strong impact. Some of his literary offspring expressed the same sense of the absurdity of human existence—for example, Samuel Beckett in *Waiting For Godot* and Tennessee Williams in *The Glass Menagerie*.

Jean-Paul Sartre's "philosophy of loneliness," however, embodied the so-called "tragic flaw" of the heroes of the great Greek, Roman and Shakespearean tragedies, such as Oedipus, Coriolanus or Macbeth, the sin of "hubris" or pride. In Sartre, the tragic flaw was the very kernel of his life-views: a disconnectedness from fellow humans so as to acknowledge neither need for nor responsibility toward them. That is hubris. That is utter loneliness.

Still, I do not condemn Sartre, nor think he is condemned. For in the midst of the suffering and the alienation of the absurdity of war, Sartre grew a compassion for the children he encountered. He was saved by the children for they called forth a sense of responsibility and the compassionate outreach which is the first step away from loneliness. This compassion for the innocent children, together with his faithful friendship with Simone de Beauvoir, a literary companion, redeemed him from the ultimate loneliness of self-imposed death. Given his philosophical mood, "the great heroism of Sartre was that he [...] did not commit suicide."[10]

Scriptural consolation

This entire book could be written on the subject of the loneliness of the artist, but we are restricting ourselves to one chapter only. It is fitting to end with some reflections on the greatest artist of all time, the consummate storyteller, the master of signs, symbols and images, the excellent illustrator, Jesus, the Christ.

He was familiar with the deepest meaning and "within-ness" of things, his Father having been the original Creator-Artisan who showed him all the models of things. Jesus taught with parables, but people did not understand and he wept. His ideas were rejected as well as his promises. In him there was no "hubris." He humbled himself and became as we are: human (Philippians 2). He told us the true story of ourselves and of God with all the connections, but even his closest disciples did not understand. In the end, he walked alone, for he knew what was in the human heart, but he was not known in return. Even today his teaching is distorted. To this lonely artist I write:

Ballad of Jesus

There was a man who told stories—
A story-telling man.
He wove stories out of lilies and bird-songs,
Told tales of trees and birds that nest in these,
Tales of pearls and fishes.
He loved water.
He loved wine.
He loved bread, the simple things.
He could take a piece of bread
And make a story of it
And what a story,
What a story he could make!
People liked to listen.
He made them feel so good
They straightened and they stood—
But failed to understand.
His parable passed over them.
Some said he was a criminal.
He stirred people, ordinary folk.
They made him climb a hill.
On the top of the hill he died.
But before he died he asked
To be remembered

And so I sing this song
In memory of Jesus.

P.S. His story did not end:
He rose to life again.

Lessening loneliness

• Recognition is not everything. Many have not been recognized in their lifetime. Don't be discouraged.

• Be true to your art as your gift. Be grateful for it and remain humble.

• You are not "above" the human race. Communicate as one of us. Art separated from life is not worthy of the name.

• Give yourself "garret time," time for reflection. But stay connected so that your story and ours are connected.

• Challenge and create as well as portray the present. True beauty brings hope and hope brings something new. We need beauty in many art forms. Believe that you touch others, unknown to you.

• Expect some suffering. Weave it into your art. It is part of every life and part of growth.

• God cannot be replaced by art nor by the artist. You share in the work of God: creating. Do it from the Source of your being, with awareness.

• The artist may be like the seer or prophet: It is a lonely role but it is essential that in that role the artist be truly in touch with both God and with people. True art is not an ego trip. If your different perception makes you feel isolated or lonely, remember it is on behalf of all. *Sym-ballein* is drawing together, *dia-ballein* is tearing apart; from these two Greek words we have "symbolic" and "diabolic." The artist's work is symbolic: it draws us together. You are one of us and one with us.

The loneliness of culture shock

Culture shock is an experience of strangeness and disorientation because of a change in location. It usually lasts a long time though it happens suddenly. Culture shock may amount to trauma. I believe it is a form of loneliness. Even in its well-known form, which we call "homesickness," it is very painful; hence the word "sickness." It can even incapacitate a person to some degree; some are more inclined to it than others. It is especially virulent if one goes alone to an unfamiliar country.

I have personally had a number of attacks of homesickness/culture shock—enough to know that I am quite susceptible. The earliest was long ago when I was a preteenager on the farm and went to spend a weekend with my girlfriend from school, Dorothy. The idea was exciting. But the reality of my first weekend away from home in unfamiliar surroundings, with parents who were not like mine, was quite unnerving. I could not sleep. My imagination became all ears for the sounds of the night. Someone snoring, which might have been a comfort to another, was disturbing to me. Breakfast was German, not like breakfast at home. There was a very old grandmother who frightened me. I did not feel like myself at all. I felt estranged and very lonely. I tried not to show how I felt so as not to seem impolite but I was literally dying to go home.

When I went to boarding school, the feeling returned and stayed with me for weeks. Part of the problem was numbers; I felt lost in a crowd. I was carried away by the routine. Where was my familiar self? Who was this stranger among strangers? I felt unknown. I believe this is the very core of loneliness itself. To feel unknown is to feel lost. All of those people and things by which we have known ourselves are gone and we are removed from our identifying "culture." One of the cures is a return visit home. This happened for me at Thanksgiving. For so many who have been forced to flee their homelands or who cannot afford a trip back, it cannot happen. I grew to love boarding school where I spent my last two years of high school, but the homesickness of the first few weeks was etched in my soul.

Far worse is culture shock in a place where the language is unfamiliar. Language is at the very heart of communication and of feeling known. Years after my boarding school experience of homesickness, I went to Quebec to visit some relatives on my father's side of the family. We had never known them, since my father had homesteaded in the West and never returned to Quebec. The West, in those days, was like China: too far away to visit.

I arrived in Quebec City, was met by strangers, none of whom spoke a word of English. We drove through unfamiliar territory, made worse by the fact that we got lost looking for my uncle's "chalet." Darkness was now falling. One of my cousins, a Franciscan sister, welcomed me to her convent. The place was part of Hôpital Sainte-Anne, a hospital for psychiatric patients, hydrocephalic children and human tragedies of various degrees. The unfamiliar sounds were quite terrifying. Because of the nature of the place, I was "locked" into my room which, in turn, was inside the locked living area. Although this "double lock" was hospital policy, it did nothing to make me feel secure. I was thoroughly unnerved and estranged. I felt physically sickened. I stood in the middle of the room and said the "Our Father" very slowly, trying to realize that all these sick and strange people were children of the same Father.

The next day, I did what had helped before, I got in touch by telephone with my father in Saskatchewan. Just hearing his voice, knowing that he knew me and knew these "strangers," hearing his familiar laugh when I told him I was homesick, dispelled some of my extreme discomfort. Perhaps it is a question of being reassured that what is familiar is still there, that all is not gone forever.

At the time of my visit, there were Americans on the moon. Sitting before the French television and grasping very little of what was said, I suddenly heard the men speaking English and relaying their messages to earth. It was an amazing experience for me. I felt closer to them than to the people in the room! They made me feel like myself again. This may all sound foolish to anyone who has not experienced culture shock; but those who have suffered it understand. I grew to appreciate the love that was in Hôpital Sainte-Anne and the tender care given to "les enfants" and the sick there. I even returned for another stay. But those first days were truly painful.

Culture shock is something one is not prepared for. I never dreamed I would experience it when I went to Quebec. After all, my parents often spoke French to each other. When maternal relatives came from northern Saskatchewan and spent a couple of days with us, our home was transformed into a French-Canadian household. We loved it; it was beautiful. But that was on location and it was at home with everything familiar. It was quite a different story for me to go alone to a place I had never seen, to be with people I had never met who spoke in a language I hardly understood. The hospital culture was, of course, the extreme in culture shift. It was not my familiars in Toronto, but my father, someone who knew and loved this city, who was able to make the link between myself and this place, so that I felt like myself again.

I returned from Quebec with a new understanding of what refugees and immigrants must go through when they come to our country. Fortunately for many, they are met and taken home by relatives or friends who preceded them. In this regard the requisite of being sponsored by someone here serves a good purpose. But for one who comes, forced to leave homeland and family milieu, arriving unknown, it must be a terrifying time even with physical needs supplied. It is summed up in the words of one person I heard say: "I have no people here." That is loneliness.

On another occasion I went with a woman from Amnesty International to visit a man who had just come alone from Uganda. He was a professor and journalist who had been imprisoned, tortured, and left for dead in the back of a truck with several others. But he had escaped: dead people are not watched. We went into the hotel room. The man was pacing up and down the room. This tall black man in a navy blue suit, who would one day be appointed Ugandan ambassador to the United Nations, was pacing like a disoriented caged animal. The TV was blaring. He knew we were coming. We introduced ourselves. We sat down. He did not sit; he continued to pace. Then seeming to become aware that this must appear odd to us, he excused himself and said:

"Please, do you mind if I move about? I feel so lost, so alone and disconnected. Thank you for coming. No, I do not need anything, just to speak with someone who knows of me."

My friend asked if she might turn the television down since it was so loud that we could scarcely hear his voice. He answered:

"Yes, of course. I didn't notice. I'm not watching it, not listening to it. I simply turned it on so as not to be all alone, so as to feel there was someone else in the room."

He had left behind his wife and family who eventually immigrated to Canada and became good neighbours to

friends of mine in Scarborough. George Wamala never got to the United Nations. He had returned to Uganda to arrange his credentials, but became ill and died in a matter of hours at thirty-nine years of age.

I remember this accomplished man in those hours of culture shock and homesickness and I saw what this form of loneliness can do to a person. I was glad to do my small part to fill that loneliness by being there, talking about his family, helping him find work as a journalist, helping him to feel someone here "knew" him and cared about him. When the new government appointed Wamala to the United Nations, it seemed like a happy ending to a story of suffering; but it was not to be. Perhaps the culture shock had taken its toll, along with the torture shock.

Torture as culture shock

Torture is another scene of extreme loneliness. I have had the opportunity to be associated with the Canadian Centre for Victims of Torture.[1] What the Centre has learned is that persons who have been imprisoned and tortured have been successfully dehumanized. They fear to tell anyone of their suffering for fear of being considered guilty of crimes. The torture has made them feel guilty in some vague way. They also fear meeting their torturers, as has actually been known to happen in our experience with the Centre. For example, when a regime falls, those who have been part of its exercise may leave the country to escape reprisal. They may even make their way as "refugees" to our country and encounter others here whom they tortured under the former regime. Such meetings are unimaginably horrifying, even if nothing more follows.

The loneliness of those who have suffered torture is hard for us to fathom. It is a terrible place, not readily opened or shared even after the persons have reached safety. One cannot cast off nightmares and they are almost impossible to share except with others who have experienced them. That is one purpose of the Centre, in addition to medical service: to safely rehumanize those who were excluded, as it were, from being human. This culture shock of exclusion from the human race is hard to cure. More than one person who has endured it has eventually committed suicide, unable to bear the memory and the imprint any longer or to tell the story one more time. It is perhaps comparable to shell-shock or war-shock which has left many a mind and body in ruins. Ruins are lonely, are they not? They tell of something grand that has been destroyed. Whatever society or the church can do to restore and rebuild the noble human beings so ruined banishes and heals one of the most acute forms of loneliness.

Refugees and immigrants

If refugees experience the most severe form of culture shock and loneliness, voluntary immigrants are not immune to this sickness. I think of J. who, in the interests of her poor family, left the Philippines and came to work in Canada. She came alone. I have known this beautiful woman for many years. She told me that it is especially at family festival times such as Christmas that the pain is very great. Her deep faith has been her standby. Not only is she consoled by the word and sacrament of God but she is impelled to reach out and do good to others who are the most alone. The Filipinos are family people. For an unmarried woman to leave her country for financial reasons and to be deprived of her close relatives is a real suffering.

Another immigrant told me:

"When I left Chile, I decided I must not come with the intention of going back 'home' as many do. That way, I shall always be homesick. No, I must make my new life here and become a new citizen."

He had his wife and family with him. Even so, he felt the pain of being located far from anyone who spoke his language. While his choice, he felt, did speed "integration," it did nothing to relieve the pain of acculturation.

Recently I watched a televised documentary on the coming of the Chinese to Western Canada in the earlier half of this century. Men came, unmarried men mostly, or men who had to leave their wives behind until they found livelihood and a place to live. These men opened "Chinese cafés" in small towns across the prairies. Those were hard times. They were isolated from each other; they were totally isolated from their culture. People ate at their cafés but left them alone or, worse, made fun of them. They were socially excluded.

Some sent back to China for wives and these came, often sight unseen. They worked seven days a week, early morning to late night, raised a family and remained culturally separate. One woman interviewed was asked if she missed China. In her reserved and shy way she said in a low voice:

"Yes. No friends here. Very lonely. [Tears welled up and she changed the subject.] But my children—I have good children, very good."

What an ache was there!

I grew up in Saskatchewan. There was a Chinese café in our village and in our town. That was "their" job, "their" place in our society, and I never dreamed of the pain of culture shock and the loneliness that these immigrants suffered. If I did not make fun of the Chinese-English tongue, at least I was completely oblivious of the pain of exclusion we were causing by not even attempting to make friends with these good neighbours who served us good food... and bore with our insults and insensitivity.

I discovered the loneliness of fellow students from other countries who came to study in London, Ottawa, Toronto. They could not afford to go home at Christmas or even in the summer. The ones that come immediately to mind are the students from Africa and from Trinidad for whom everything was different from home: food, climate, clothing, customs, ways of relating to family and other people, and study methods. Fortunately, they knew the language. Being in small groups with them for classes, meals and recreation, some of us began to sense their loneliness and to speak of our differences. Their needs were different and we had been insensitive to them.

On the other hand, H., who came from Trinidad, simply withdrew more and more. He grew thinner and thinner until some of us became alarmed and spoke to one of the professors about him. The professor happened to be Sister Corinne of the French Department. She drew him aside one morning after class. As soon as she opened the subject of how he was feeling, H. burst into tears. He had in fact been very hungry, trying to make ends meet, trying to do two semesters in one in order to shorten his exile and make funds stretch. There had been no one to whom he felt he could confide his difficulties or his heartache. That was the worst part—the heartache. Once the secrecy of the loneliness had been broken with at least some of us, things began to improve. H. successfully completed his stay here. A few years later, a friend, who went to live in Trinidad and whom I had put in touch with H., told a very different story of a happy, hearty, and very welcoming H. contacted "at home."

Loneliness of those who return "home"

Strange to relate, the culture shock, homesickness and loneliness of refugees and immigrants is often experienced in reverse by persons returning to their homeland after years in another country. In particular, missionaries who have gone and stayed in countries of the Southern Hemisphere, living in solidarity with struggling peoples, experiencing the poverty but also the community bonds, find it difficult to re-adapt to a country such as Canada or the United States. The people of their adopted country have become "my people" for them. The culture shock is all the more acute because people here cannot imagine why anyone would not be very glad to return to "civilization." There can be a real sense of dislocation and inability to re-adapt with no desire to do so.

The returnees are affronted by the wealth and apparent callousness or blindness they find among us. They are shocked by the lack of understanding, the oblivion about the gaps between countries. They feel unknown, as it were. "I am not the person you know, not the same person I was when I left," they tell us. In a way, they are misfits. But they do not wish to appear ungrateful by expressing the pain that is in them. There is a centre in Canada for the reculturation of returned missionaries comparable to training centres such as Maryknoll which prepare missionaries to go abroad.

A returning missionary speaks for herself in this letter she wrote about a month after she and her companions had to leave Guatemala. They were "on the list," the "fichadas," with threats to their lives and the lives of those with whom they worked:

> As you can see by the address, I'm in Canada. I left Guatemala by plane December 16th, accompanied by the four sisters with whom I'd been missioned. [...]
>
> I wanted to write to you sooner, but just couldn't seem to settle down to it, until today. Presently, I'm busy coping with my own inner feelings of pain, sadness, loneliness, disappointment and anger. I suddenly find myself ripped away and completely separated

from the people I'd shared life with so deeply over the last eleven years. People who so simply, openly and lovingly welcomed me into their lives. Together we shared our daily struggles, joys, weaknesses and sorrows. Now cut off from them, I feel so utterly naked, stripped, empty and alone. I hurt all over.

I now realize how deeply I love them and how very committed I'd been to them over the years, as I tried to accompany them in their struggle for justice and freedom. It's been a great blessing and privilege.[...] They have enriched my being, evangelized me as they brought me to a deeper, clearer understanding of Jesus and his message of love—Jesus poor and suffering, giving his life for me.

(Sister Trudy)

For so many returning missionaries and workers, the goals and interests of our culture no longer hold any attraction. They often prefer not to adjust fully but to find other places and peoples with whom they are more at home. In any case, the period of return is a lonely time.

Jay's story

When I think of overcoming the loneliness of culture shock, I think of a young man from Pondicherry, India, whom I met on December 18, 1987. His name is Jayaraman, Jay for short. In 1986, International Year of Peace, Jay undertook to cycle for peace. He was studying engineering at university when he heard a speaker who moved him to find a way to work for peace. He decided to take time from his studies and cycle throughout India to draw attention to the urgency of disarmament. This completed, Jay decided to cycle around the world. He was about midway on his journey when I met him in Toronto. He was not asking for money but for sponsoring letters and for hospitality. He will take all these letters to the United Nations at the end of his journey.

Jay is only twenty-two years old. He is small, gentle and pleasant of manner. He had already been to

Afghanistan, Laos, Burma, Thailand, Bangladesh, Malaysia, Singapore, Australia, Argentina, Uruguay, Brazil, Venezuela, Cuba, Jamaica, Mexico, the United States, and Canada. He would soon be on his way to Europe, Africa and Moscow, returning by air to the United Nations. Impressed by his initiative, the Indian Government paid his airfares between continents.

I looked at this youth with the peaceable face and I had to ask him:

"You have been travelling in so many strange lands and cultures. Do you sometimes get homesick?"

He told me that, since he had started by travelling in his own country, he was able in the first weeks to keep in touch with his family quite easily. "Still, there are numerous cultures and languages in India." He speaks six languages: English, Hindi, Telgu, Tamil, Canadam and Malayalan.

"At first, I was homesick. Gradually, I learned that all families are my family. Under all is the human family. We are the same everywhere."

Jay had met many cultures in India but he had also met with a refusal of entry to Pakistan, divided from India on religious grounds. Jay's journey required a great deal of trust in strangers and much courage. In one country he was robbed. In Brazil, communication was difficult; but with a few basic words and the willing help of police stations and communities, he could continue to make his way. He had been through the long miles of the Australian outback. Only at his country's embassies could he reconnect with his family by mail.

Jay had overcome homesickness and loneliness in the cause of peace. He had discovered a truth that can actually cure loneliness: we are all one. He had great courage to go alone and to be alone. Jay is probably somewhere in Europe now, cycling along its roads heading toward Africa, knocking on doors with the air of a holy innocent, bringing peace and calling it forth, bearing his witness to the unity of the human family.

Culture shock of the native peoples, the transient, the poor

Even within a country, people can suffer the loneliness of culture shock. Native people who leave their reserve and come to the city feel it. Are they ever "at home"? Having spent several summers with the Ojibway people of Sheshegwaning, West Bay and Wikwemikong Reserves, I have seen the difference between home on the reserve and home in the city. I am not speaking of the physical poverty or amenities, but of being "at home." There, "we have our people"; here: "I have no people." No people in the sense of a planted, rooted, or belonging people in command of their lives and their space. On the reserve, they know each other's "kids" and speak their own language. But often they are strangers in their own land in our cities. For that matter, are they not in some way strangers in their own land throughout this country inasmuch as their original homeland is no longer theirs? There is a loneliness and a longing for a return to their own culture and arts, including their own religious culture, their spiritual "home."

Perhaps it is expressed best in this small poem:

Seeking Manitou

He sees geese
Flowing south
In V's

October spilling
Colour on the leaves

Yearning to be
With them

Flying
Crying

Trying to find
Manitou

Before winter.....

(Norman Sommer)

Families on the move, youngsters changing schools, loss of proximity to extended family all make for at least a mild form of culture shock and loneliness. Then there is the cultural division of rich and poor or simply middle class and street people. It appears at times as if these are two different species. We have all walked around an unkempt, unwashed person on the street, chosen our seat on the subway to avoid an "undesirable" or even avoided public transportation entirely because of the "types" one meets there.

In small communities, the likelihood is that the neighbours would rally to help. In larger cities, the poor remain anonymous and excluded. They may have financial means offered them but they are not part of the culture of the rich. It takes only a glance to establish the disconnection, a glance that says the other is not of my category, not quite human.

I recorded two experiences in my New York journal that illustrate the kind of culture shock and loneliness I have just outlined. They might have happened anywhere.

On the eve of the opening of the General Assembly of the United Nations, a prayer service was held in the Holy Family Church, the Catholic parish church of the United Nations. A reception followed the service, which was more like a concert with young musicians featured. Many UN ambassadors and staff were present as well as high level churchmen.

As refreshments were being served, a knight of the road joined us. Only he did not really join us. No one acknowledged his presence. He took a coffee and a handful of cakes and moved off to the side of the room. For most of those gathered it seemed he was not there at all. No one "knew" him. I walked over with my coffee, began to converse with him and found him to be human! He had enjoyed the music very much; he was knowledgeable about classical music. We discussed the young violinist who was without doubt a prodigy. He was knowledgeable about classical music. He thanked me for talking with him.

The other example I entitle "Sunday Service." I am not proud of my part in this story:

> As I waited in the church vestibule for the 12:10 liturgy to end, a man of about thirty came in, hunched, unkempt and coughing. I did not want to stare but I though he was a man in need. Just then the people came pouring out of the church and the man disappeared within.
>
> I entered the church and settled near the front. I noticed "him" sitting two seats over. I recall what followed as if it were happening now:
>
> The acolytes are busy setting up for the 1:15, removing the last collection, adjusting microphones. The liturgy begins. I glance at "him" and see he is scratching and hear him coughing. Coughing and scratching! Probably lousy! The couple near him moves over. I have a sense that everyone is ignoring him. Maybe he'll go away. But he is like a sore in the House of God, a sore for all to see and yet no one sees. But then, I must not judge. Am I not one of them?
>
> The homily begins. I am thinking: I will give him the money I brought for the collection, the lunch in my bag and, of course, my advice. In the middle of the homily and of my thoughts, "he" gets up abruptly, walks down the aisle and out the door, an alien figure preaching us his own sermon.
>
> We, especially I, have failed to welcome the stranger, to communicate to him that we know he is one of us.

As this man walked down the aisle, I thought he was a lonely man indeed. He was a man excluded. Perhaps in the beginning he was somewhat to blame. Perhaps many cannot empathize with the things written in this chapter because they have never experienced these things. Still, to be aware of the loneliness of others may enable us to alleviate it in some way. We may be able to reach out to another, to acknowledge the person there and help make him feel at home.

Scriptural consolation

In Judaism, it is enjoined upon the people by God to be good to the stranger, because "you were once strangers in the land of Egypt." No one is to molest the newcomer in any way. The Book of Ruth is a tender story of a Gentile woman faithful to the mother of her Jewish husband after his death. Ruth leaves her homeland to accompany her mother-in-law back to her people. There Ruth is a stranger, but she is allowed to glean from the fields and is finally accepted into the family of her deceased husband. She is an ancestor of Jesus, the Christ.

One of the most touching psalms expresses the loneliness we have been considering in this part. Psalm 137 (136) has been the basis of many a song.

> Beside the rivers of Babylon
> We sat down and wept at the memory of Zion.
> Leaving our harps hanging on the poplar trees.

Their captors asked them to sing their songs for them:

> How could we sing for them
> The songs of Zion
> Far from Jerusalem
> In a pagan land?

Egypt was also a symbol of the people's exile and slavery. The return to the promised land was and is at the very heart of Judaism, the experience of being a people, God's people. It was to Egypt that Joseph fled with Mary and the threatened Child. There they must have longed for their home, wondering when it would be safe to return, waiting for news. That must have been culture shock for them.

In some sense, we all long for our homeland for "we have here no lasting city" (Hebrews 13:14). But while we are here, we can comfort one another and make our home a place where people are known, make our homeland a welcoming one.

Lessening loneliness

• Try to "be where you are." Decide to live as fully as you can where you have to be now, rather than long for and idealize the place you have left.

.• Seek out others. If you have been a refugee or a newcomer, reach out to the new ones and help them feel at home, remembering you were once a stranger. If returning "home" you feel like a misfit, seek out others who feel the same way. Find new places to share your life. It may not be desirable to "adjust": your loneliness may be prophetic to us.

• Find a group, a support group or a church group who will be trustworthy and aid you in entering a new culture. Helpers, stick with people over time; your commitment is very important.

• Ask questions. Learn basic words first if the language is new. Try to speak. Your eyes, signs, and so forth will help you communicate.

• All of us are one human family, no matter how different. The differences are not degrees of humanness or civilization as we sometimes think. Show interest.

• Respect the fact that we tend to fear what we do not know. You fear the other but the other also fears you. Fear can be lessened by communication.

• This kind of loneliness will lessen with time.

• Street persons who appear dirty and dehumanized frighten us. But they reflect something in us and they are brother and sister to us. To the street person: as far as possible, pay attention to cleanliness and civil language so that you do not distance ordinary people from you. We know there are beggars who have been canonized saints. We know God walks with the poor and what we do to each other, we do to God.

• If you know the "Our Father," pray it slowly and include all of us who are in God's creative care and knowledge. Life is one, a gift to each of us, no matter where or how we are.

Bottled loneliness

I live at Matt Talbot House, a "dry" residence for older alcoholic men. Many people are familiar with the name of Matt Talbot, the small, wiry Irishman, a saintly alcoholic who is now "Venerable." Matt Talbot's father and brothers were a drinking lot. He began to drink at the age of twelve with his first job in a wine-bottling store. By the age of 28, heavy drinking had become his preoccupation. He had no interest in the wrestling, card-playing, dancing or partying of his friends. His one drive was to make money for drink. He even sometimes pawned his boots and came home barefoot.

One day, penniless and thirsty, Matt Talbot waited outside a public house where some of his buddies were buying drink, in the hope and expectation that one of them would surely "stand him a drink." No one offered. He turned and went home sober. He took the pledge and never took another drink. It was the beginning of a holy and disciplined life. The drinking ended but the struggle never ceased.

Was it that moment of extreme loneliness at the pub door that led Matt Talbot to turn to his Higher Power? Matt remained more or less a loner all his life. But his faithfulness to prayer, his discipline and his concern for fellow-workers and family turned that loneness into a life that still inspires many.

Here at Matt Talbot House where about twenty men live, we try to be a community, sharing meals, recreation and work. We try to support one another to remain sober. Some of the men have contact with family; others have little or none. They are mainly alone. Most of them know well what loneliness is. Part of that loneliness is the loss of family, home, ability to work, and, I suspect, "respectability" in the eyes of the public. It is not easy to know the men well, probably in part because their self-image is low and fragile (like all of us, they protect it). They do not easily reveal their inner selves—an essentially lonely way to be. I suspect this lonely way of being did not follow their alcoholism but preceded it. Their "cure" for loneliness only led to a life out of control.

A gentle exterior usually covers a great deal of anger in an alcoholic person. Who of us has not passed on the street a drunk man or woman cursing and swearing aloud, very angry at no one in particular but at everyone in general—or at life in general! We tend to shun and run. But if we are honest, we may admit that, in the face of failure, betrayal, continued frustration or simply the immensity of evil, we have felt like doing the same. We are lonely when we feel beaten. The drunk person is releasing the long pent-up anger at what he cannot control, whether the drink or life itself. We run from our own image when we run from him. He or she is alone and unable to cope. We only hope we can cope better.

The loneliness of the alcoholic has been brought home to me many times. Recently a new friend of mine, a recovering alcoholic with seven years of sobriety, told me:

"One morning, I woke up and as I lay there, I thought, 'God, I'm lonely! I am completely alone. I have drunk myself into absolute isolation. No one is with me now. No one! This is not human. No one has done this to me, I have done it to myself and it is not human.' I lay there stunned. The realization was so painful and so overpowering that it shocked me into a decision. I could not go on like this.

"The memory of that extreme loneliness which separated me from the human race continues to help me not only to sobriety but to community."

He proceeded at that time to seek out a spiritual guide, to make a retreat, and, following that, to find some manual work which would be a service to others. This he found as a caretaker for a multicongregational church.

One man who lived with us here experienced a loneliness I remember like an etching. He was talented with his hands, made a real contribution to the well-being of the house, gave us much fun with his wit. But he was unable to remain sober for more than a few weeks at a time. Just before he would go drinking an immense sadness would come over him. One could see it, feel it, but never touch it. It seemed to me I knew what loneliness really was when I looked at him in these moments. His head, which was rugged and handsome, seemed fallen, overcome. His eyes full of pain. I suppose he could not believe how much we would miss him. One hopes that such a man, so many such men, will at least one day know that they have neither to hide nor run from their hurting self, or feel alone in a group.

Another alcoholic man does not live here but often finds his way to our threshold. He seems to be invited by the warm spot of light in the tiny porch between the outside door and the inner one. There we find him again and again. I think he likes us, even when he is very drunk. The men call him "Irish." I think he likes the warm light but also the attention we give him, the saying of his nickname as if we "knew" him. We have to ask him to leave and go to his own room up the street. We try to do this respectfully and with persuasion and he is never nasty to us. Somehow this man is the embodiment of loneliness, drawn to the light of our doorway and to others inside who will come out to him. It's not that he is so conscious of it (sometimes he is hardly conscious at all!), but I feel this about him, I wonder who else he has. I don't know.[1]

Encounter with Leroy

Already ten years ago I encountered this loneliness of the alcoholic. Let me recount the story just as I recorded it in my journal. I was hurrying home from my work at Shoppers' Drop-In on Yonge Street. As I passed St. Andrew's church I noticed a man sitting on the steps on the inner sidewalk. He was asking for money. I brushed past like everyone else thinking, "One can't stop and give money to every transient." I walked briskly on to the overpass at Jarvis doing this mental justification as I went, but feeling powerfully drawn back as if the man were addressing me by name. I found myself asking myself, "Have you nothing to give him—not silver or gold—but nothing else?"

Then I turned around and walking back I approached the man and he asked me if I had any change I could give him. I bent down and told him I very much wanted to give him something else.

"What is that?"

"Something that would make you not have to sit here asking for money."

He was immensely beautiful in my eyes at that moment, like an expectant child. We began to converse, he and I. He said the police told him they would take him down to Cherry Beach. There was fear in his words.

"What's Cherry Beach? Will they throw me in the water?"

"No, I don't think so."

"If they hurt me, if they beat my head on the sidewalk...we shouldn't do that, should we? That's not God's laws, is it?"

He was drunk but he remembered.

"No, that's not God's law. It's not the law at all."

Then: "Do you think alcoholics are criminals?"

"No. But they may do some wrong things, maybe to get money."

"Are men born evil? Do you think I'm evil?" (He went from the general to the particular—himself.)

"No, you are a very beautiful man. You are God's creation and God made you good. I wish you could believe that so you would not need to run from yourself."

"Two girls went by here and they said: 'Jesus loves you.' Does he love me?"

"Yes. And he wants to give you life."

"I heard that he knocks but he can't come in unless we open the door. I guess I haven't opened the door yet. But if God loves me, why is there so much evil in this world?" (Back to life in general again!)

He asked all the questions that I ask over and over. He was so much like me!

"It is we who make evil. God made us free and we can do evil to one another. We can choose to go this way or the other way."

"That's what my mother told me when I was fourteen. Do you think I'm evil? It's addiction. God hates what I'm doing."

"Only because it is destroying you, and God loves you and does not want you to be destroyed. You are enslaved and I wish you could be free and I know Jesus can free you if you can trust him with your life. You're caught, aren't you?"

"I'm a beggar. Am I a beggar?"

"That's not so bad. Peter and John were going into the Temple and they met a man who was a beggar. He couldn't walk and used to sit and ask for money just like you do. He asked Peter and John, and Peter said, 'I have no silver or gold. But what I have I give you. In the name of Jesus get up and walk.'"

"Did he get up and walk?"

"Yes."

There was a pause, a silence.

Then the man began to speak of the police again. He was afraid of the police.

"The police say they protect people. But sometimes they hurt people. That's not the law. Is it the law when they hurt people?"

"They do what they think they have to do. But sometimes they don't do the law either. We have to have some laws to live together in a big city and sometimes people don't keep the law."

"You're a Christian woman, aren't you?"

"Yes. And I think that you are not far from the kingdom of God. You are a good man. Jesus identifies himself with people like you. He says we visit him when we visit someone in the hospital. If we go to see someone in prison, we are going to see him. That's what he said. He wants to free you and give you his gifts. I wish you could trust him to help you. He knows. He's human like you."

There was silence to let this sink in.

Then I said, "I have to go now." I gave him some money then. He changed the subject, wanting me to stay.

"Why does God send storms and rain?" (It had been raining for days and days and he was cold.)

"The earth needs rain to give us food. It seems bad when you are wet and cold, but the rain is good."

"Yes."

"Good-bye now."

He put out his hand. I took it. At that moment I realized that I had been quite unaware of the crowds passing by. There was just "him and me." He was looking deep into me. He was handsome, well-built, with dark heavy hair and searching eyes.

"I love you."

"I love you, too." (For I had truly conceived a love for him in my heart.)

He wept. And I wept. It began to rain again.

He got up quickly then and walked westward. I walked, ran, eastward, wondering that Jesus Christ had revealed himself to me sitting on the sidewalk steps. Who am I that he should show me his face?... that I should look into his eyes and recognize him in his loneliness?

I think that every person who puts out a hand asking for some change as you pass by, no matter how unworthy we may think they are, is really asking for a human communication, a word, a look of respect. The Eastern spiritual writer Evagrius says: Every human face is an icon of Christ. Sometimes the icon is badly damaged. But under the appearance is the loneliness and our common humanity.

According to Ox and Harvey

After writing part of this chapter, I decided to ask "Ox," the pseudonym of one of the men at Matt Talbot who dabbles in writing himself, to read what I had written, to make some comments on it, and to tell his own story, if he so wished. He gave me the following, handwritten:

> Most alcoholics have two conflicting traits or emotions—that of being lonely and that of wanting privacy or anonymity. We take what is called the "geographic" cure: moving from place to place, trying to escape the failures and despair of our past.
>
> We cover our moves with self-deception—the "grass is greener on the other coast" or "I want to get away from my drinking buddies." This means that all chances of repaying debt or fighting others' hostility are gone.
>
> Escape! The geographic cure! until the next time. The constant moving negates the chances of close ties, until out of despair they are avoided completely.
>
> Hence, the loneliness is all-surrounding. The family is gone. First, friends shut the door, then parents, the wife or husband, then the children.

If the disease starts at an early age, the sufferer and the children cannot bond in any sort of relationship. There is only about a 20% chance of any reconciliation.

Having no permanent relationship certainly leads to loneliness. The need for privacy, or withdrawal, is paramount in most cases. We shut out emotional contact. A lot of us will try remarriage two or even three times as another escape from the past.

Not until we face our problems—honestly—can we begin to assimilate into an acceptable lifestyle.

We are going to carry our hurt all the rest of our lives—our guilt and our failure.

The alternatives are a restructuring of our lives, or continued loneliness, or suicide. The alternatives are dreaded in any case, because of the chance of failing again and leaving nothing but continued drinking and death as a way out.

Friends, family, God have left the drinking person's life, even though they dominate a lot of conversations. It takes outside help from professionals and other forms of treatment to steer the sufferer back to normalcy.

The first most likely to reappear is the religious life. Friends and family may never accept the "reborn" back again, and that is a stalling point in ever attempting to recover.

It takes more than willpower to overcome this illness. It takes the dedicated help of all alcoholic support groups.

So withdrawal and the accompanying loneliness are a way of life—if it can be called that!

Ox

I also approached Harvey whom I have known for some years at Matt Talbot House and asked him if he would be willing to be interviewed for this book.

"Sure, I'll be glad to help you out," he agreed. He came over after supper on that Sunday night. At first he was not sure if "loneliness" was the right word for his experience. But as we talked, Harvey used the word several times, in some form or other. He started by referring to mornings:

"The worst is in the morning, if I'm not going to work. If I'm going to work I don't have time to think about it. But I hate Sundays. Like this morning, I wanted to phone Charlie, but you can't call someone who's sleeping in on a Sunday morning. I feel a sort of void on days I don't work, like being stuck.

"Of course, I can be lonely in a crowd, feel I don't fit. I sometimes feel I don't fit. I'm better one to one rather than in a crowd. I'm a quiet person. I wonder if people who are really loud are happy or covering up."

I agreed that often it may be a cover-up to clown and be loud. ("Was he referring to me?" I wondered in passing. I am sometimes called "Noisy" for short!) Harvey went on, telling me how "big cities can be lonely." Then I asked him what picture or image comes to mind when I say the word "loneliness." He answered:

"A poem comes to mind:

Along the line of smokey hills
The crimson forest stands;
And all day long the blue jay calls
Throughout the autumn lands.[2]

"Robbie Burns has some poems that are lonely, too. That can be a beautiful scene. But I've experienced being in the bush at a cottage. If you're with someone it's a nice scene, but if you're all alone, stuck there in the bush, that can be a lonely scene. No company. You're stuck. Maybe there's a certain fear.

"I love the country but I couldn't be alone. It's not that I'm longing for someone in particular but just to be with someone. I don't like being alone.

"Another lonely picture would be a group of people in a room, maybe around a table, and one person over in the corner—they're not part of it. I can be happy being quiet. I like thinking and not having people bug me. But I want other people around me in the house."

Harvey is not the first to associate loneliness with a vague kind of fear. He told me how his father and two brothers had died within about a year.

"It left me with a certain fear—like being left alone." This same feeling of fear-loneliness had become familiar to Harvey in other circumstances of being left:

"I loved having a gang of kids around the house, with their friends. It was good coming home to that. Then it was gone. I suppose kids have to grow up and leave. But I came home one day and my furniture was gone and my wife. And she had the little girl with her. That was really lonely. To lose a child is really worse than losing anyone else. I used to walk down the street and if I saw a little blonde girl I would stop and look to see if it was her. Your family hides from you and that really feels lonely. I'm a possessive person. I don't know if it's jealousy or what."

I offered that it might be insecurity. Harvey proceeded:

"My wife had got me a little book, once, with pictures and words to go with them. It was a nice thing. I remember one page especially that said: 'Missing you before you leave.' I never forgot that.

"I used to miss friends and buddies who would go off to cottages or to work some place for the summer. One friend used to go to Vancouver and I said: 'What do you have to go way out there for?' I never liked spring and summer because people went away.

"But then sometimes I got into relationships and wanted to break off so I'd go and get drunk and the person would leave. That would be the end of it and it would all be over. Then when you start sobering up and while you're sobering up, it's sort of exciting because you're working at it and making progress. Then, the longer you're sober, the more complacent you become until it starts all over again."

I did not understand what Harvey was saying so I questioned him,

"What do you mean—'you get complacent'?"

"Well, I mean you get more and more to reality. Then like I said, in the morning it hits you, a sort of frantic loneliness, early when you wake up, because reality hits and you know you've got nothing left."

I could feel the pain in the expression Harvey used: "frantic loneliness." Reality is often a healing comfort to persons suffering loss. But for the alcoholic "reality" represents total loss, even, in a sense, loss of a future. In another way though, reality is the only "salvation" because it is the starting point for the decision to seek help perseveringly. It is required as the ground for attaining and maintaining sobriety. Reality and truth are the foundation of the never-ending struggle.

Harvey is gifted in music and in the use of his hands to make things. I have a fine upholstered prayer stool and a sturdy music stand as proof. He is a creative person. I asked him what helps him most in combatting loneliness, and he answered,

"I need a project—even at work I think up something, like maybe helping people keep track of tools." Harvey continued:

"I like to think, come up with some positive ideas and how they can work. People think I'm withdrawn but I enjoy thinking.

"The phone is a big help. Of course, at Matt Talbot, I don't want to tie up the phone too long so that can be a problem. I don't like to call somebody and then have to tell them I have to hang up. I like to talk a good long time."

I asked Harvey my usual question, "What advice would you give to an alcoholic person—supposing the person isn't as creative as you are?"

Without a moment's hesitation Harvey answered:

"Go to AA. Take an address book and take down as many numbers as you can get. Call next day and verify if they're really interested in keeping in touch. The phone is a very big help. There's no reason to sit around feeling lonely.

"Also, get a hobby. Music has been a hobby for me when I had the keyboard, but it could be anything. There's lots of things to do, places to go. You don't need to be bored either. I'm not bored.

"But then sometimes I just don't move. Like today when you called me to ask if I'd do this interview, I was sleeping because it was Sunday and I don't like Sundays."

Need for human support, the ability to face death

We wound up our conversation and I felt I understood just a little better the loneliness experienced by alcoholics. Harvey also noted that, when he goes drinking, he goes looking for other people, someone to talk to, who also wants someone to talk to. But, of course, such contacts are not lasting. When the drink takes its toll, the communication breaks down, sociability is gone and isolation takes over once more.

There is evidence of this desire for human relationship in the fact that alcoholics often want to "share" with a buddy or two the bottled comfort. Add to that the phenomenon of the amazing grapevine system among them, of the whereabouts and condition of each.

Finally, I have been deeply impressed again and again as we have accompanied men through their dying, how serenely, how realistically they approach death, perhaps more so than they approached life. They seem to have had so much practice at living a life beyond control that now they can quietly surrender to the process of dying which is certainly beyond control. Their anger spent, as it were, they are neither morose nor fearful, but seem to have a sort of confidence. They have learned what we all have to learn: that we cannot really count on ourselves. God is going to have to save us after all. Furthermore, the loneliness of dying and of death seems to them almost like a familiar companion, nothing new... just the last loneliness. The serenity prayer seems then to have been answered.

Maybe I seem to be idealizing the men. I am only writing what I have observed in them and what has edified me. Maybe I am edified because I have to pray often that I will not go out kicking and screaming, rebelling against the way it is, as I have too often rebelled in life; but rather that I will go humbly to God in my death.

The loneliness of spouses, family, friends

The woman who has tried to live and cope with an alcoholic husband (or the man who has struggled through many years of hell with an alcoholic wife) will indeed wonder how I can write in this way about alcoholics. I am not forgetting the loneliness these spouses and their families have had, trying to defend, protect, cover for the alcoholic, and to hide the situation from relatives and the public. Nor do I forget that the loneliness of the alcoholic is full of self-pity. They themselves admit it. The loneliness nonetheless remains. I invite those who have suffered immeasurably from the behaviour of an alcoholic spouse to remember not only the pain but the attractiveness that person once held for her or him and the love once felt, and to realize that the size of the problem of alcoholism is larger than the bottle.

The abuse of alcohol, which at first seems to make us friendly but in the end isolates us from friends and family, is a cry for a relationship with God and with others. Yet the same ones who cry for this lasting community of life seem most unable to have it. They seem to have needs others are unable to fill. Are their expectations too high? Is their loneliness too great for what life has to offer? Living requires a certain humility before its mystery. It requires a certain ability to live well without having all the answers. It requires that we accept our uniqueness even while this makes us lonely. In a sense, our loneliness is the result of our specialness which somehow sets us apart from all others. The paradox is that we all experience loneliness and this makes us all very much alike, very human.

The damage done to alcoholics, their spouses and children is serious and requires much healing. There are now not only Al-Anon and Alateen groups, but ACAPs, groups for Adult Children of Alcoholic Parents. All of these "victims" can avail themselves of the helps to their great hurt and loneliness. They need to know "you are not alone." Their loneliness may be less obvious than the ravaged face and uncoordinated feet of the alcoholic—which are the very image of loneliness and the attempt to escape it. If my friend diagnosed that his isolation, made complete by the drinking, was not human, then communication with God, our Higher Power, and with others in a community of life (or whatever mix) is part of the way of recovery and of becoming human again.

Scriptural consolation

The problem of intoxication goes a long way back. After the flood, we read that "Noah, a tiller of soil, was the first to plant a vine" (Genesis 9:18ff.). He drank some of the wine and, while drunk, lay naked in his tent. His youngest son, Ham, found his father in this condition. He went out and described it to his two brothers, evidently making fun of or showing contempt toward his father. The other two went and covered Noah with a cloak, holding it up so as not to look on their father's drunken nakedness. One could say that people, especially children of alcoholics, have been "covering up" ever since. When Noah sobered up, he cursed Ham and blessed the other two sons. The point is that we are not to lose respect for the person of the alcoholic, as Ham did. This is a person with a progressive disease that causes much pain and humiliation.

Jesus was accused of eating and drinking with publicans and sinners, of communicating with prostitutes and street people, who he said would enter the kingdom of God before many, especially before the rich; in fact, Jesus said it was harder for a rich person to enter the kingdom of God than for a camel to go through the eye of a needle. But Jesus followed that remark with one that must surely be consoling to the alcoholic who feels small hope of a cure. Jesus

said: "For humans it is impossible, but with God nothing is impossible" (Luke 18:27).

Jesus also used examples, such as putting new wine in new wineskins and the story of the prodigal son, to indicate that the situation of the down-and-out can be redeemed to new life. Change can happen. He urged us to invite to our table not those who can repay the favour but those who cannot. In his parable of the reign of God as a great banquet, Jesus says those invited would not come and so their places will be taken by those in the highways and biways, the lonely street people. He said it is not those who are well who need the doctor but those who are sick. And that is why he came.

I have discovered the paschal mystery in the lives of the alcoholic men I have known at Matt Talbot House, my home. The story of Jesus is the story of life, death and resurrection... that is, the paschal mystery. One day, Paul, who had left us, came back to the house battered and bruised from a bout of drinking. He was very discouraged.

"I'm no good!" he said, shaking his head. "I'll never be any good."

I said to him truthfully, "Paul, when I look at you I see Jesus in his death and resurrection, over and over again, falling and rising. Keep going." He wept and I hoped he would always remember.

The alcoholic usually ends up being alone, if not physically at least emotionally. Long long ago it was written that God said, "It is not good for man to be alone" (Genesis 1:18). It tells of our human need to have companions in community of life. As Ecclesiastes (Qoheleth) put it:

> Woe to the man by himself
> with no one to help him up when he falls down.
>
> (Qoheleth 4:10)

To paraphrase: "Woe to the woman by herself with no one to help her up when she falls down."

The first Christians formed communities of faith to live the gospel in the face of social and cultural difficulties and persecution. Both the healthy and the sick need a community to strengthen the weary arms and the flagging knees. Let the alcoholic sick person know that there is a community of people desiring his or her wellness and willing to help, knowing all things are possible with God.

Lessening loneliness

• No one sets out to be an alcoholic. No one wants the disastrous side effects of alcohol or other drugs. And no one can return from the lonely path until he or she admits that life is out of control. It is not a question of when, where, how or even why one is drinking, but of what it is doing to my life? The starting point is reality. That is what the so-called "Serenity Prayer" is about:

> God, grant me
> the serenity to accept the things I cannot change,

the courage to change the things I can,
and the wisdom to know the difference.

Reality is: the alcoholic, by willpower, cannot change the *fact* that he or she is an alcoholic. But the way life is lived out can be changed.

• Do not try to go it alone. No one can.

• Use *Alcoholics Anonymous*. I cannot improve on it. One of the first sentences I ever read in a pamphlet of AA was: *You are not alone*. The fellowship of AA is all important.

• Try to find a house or community group to share life with if you are living alone or on the street. This must be a group with an understanding of the disease and a lifestyle of sobriety. If you are in your family, get addiction counselling as a family.

• Trust your Higher Power, not your own willpower, remembering you are never left alone.

• Families and friends of alcoholics: go to Al-Anon, Alateen or ACAP (Adult Children of Alcoholic Parents) to help yourself on the lonely path. You are not alone either. You may also get help to confront with love the denying alcoholic person so as to really enable that person to take the first step. The best way to help and support an alcoholic is *not* to cover up but to face the truth.

• With the Higher Power, all things are possible, nothing is impossible.

Alienation: The lonely psyche

We are familiar with psychiatric ills. The term covers a wide range of disturbances from inner conflict through mild and varied neuroses to breakdowns and psychoses. Most people suffer from some form of neurosis: a phobia such as fear of flying, fear of heights, elevators or dark tunnels. The neurosis might be a habit of negative thinking: always the worst first! It might be a depression from time to time, an addiction to caffeine or nicotine to help us cope, an "ennui" during which we feel "fedup" with life. We all experience degrees of alienation from other people, ourselves or even God at times. Such alienation, though temporary, causes immense suffering and great loneliness of spirit. Simone Weil writes of what she names "affliction," a sort of inconsolable heartache that has to be lived through. The extreme form of alienation is suicide. The loneliness caused by psychiatric ills is a subject we need to look at in this book.

So many of us know the neurotic, repetitive patterns of thought which come to plague us when things are not going well. Sister Gwen calls these the "tapes" that seem to

play in our heads. She replays for us one of her own "tapes" in the following transcript:

"I over-prepared for this meeting to ward off criticism. It has backfired: all my careful details evoke great annoyance. The person in charge says: 'Did no one ever tell you you can't communicate?'

"Of course. But I thought I was making myself clear. Tears threaten to spill over and I can't speak. Both of us back off.

"On the way home, I feel so uneasy about myself. I wish someone could explain to me why I react like this. My 'no nonsense' voice within reproaches me with: 'This whole thing is silly. Such a production over nothing!' But somewhere in me is this cry-baby child that I fear is the real me. My head tells me Jesus is present but that only makes his absence from my feelings all the more painful. I can't pray. I weep but it doesn't touch the lonely spot.

"I try to stay with the pain, to reach a breakthrough. I turn to Jesus asking, 'When did you feel like this?' but the answer seems to be: 'Never! You think God would be so petty?' Again, a wave of utter loneliness.

"Now the memory of being five years old: I come crying to my mother that the big kids will not let me play with them. I recall her words: 'Stop crying or I'll give you something to cry for.' The lump of utter loneliness and disapproval rises in my chest again.

"It's late. I drift off to sleep wishing I could dig this out once and for all.

"Next day, with the tape still playing, I go, heavy, tired, resisting, to the parish. The person who triggered the tape replay is there, having a misunderstanding with someone else. Tempers flare. I resist the temptation to gloat! Instead, compassion and prayer for reconciliation come through.

"We begin with the scripture reading of the day. It tells of Jesus heading resolutely for Jerusalem. The leader writes on the board: Jesus, cornerstone, shalom-peace.

"Into my mind leaps the phrase: 'The stone which the builders rejected has become the cornerstone.'

"'Rejected!' My feeling is truly named. I know I am understood—perfectly, by Jesus. The tape turns off. This time, the tears are gratitude. There is a moment of intimate presence...

"I have passed through the trap door of my false self to a new depth I haven't yet sounded."

We know our own "tapes." We may have learned how to turn them off or we may need help to learn, so that the tapes are not allowed to control our lives and alienate us from others. They can cause a failure in real communication that results in a sense of rejection, misunderstanding and loneliness.

Fear is another familiar "ill." In its best sense, when well-founded, fear can protect us from harm. We would be rash to try to ignore it. In its domineering form, it can prevent us from living a free and well-adjusted life and lead us to a certain isolation and loneliness. In the form of human respect coupled with a low self-image, it may inhibit us from relating with others or doing what we would like to do. The consequence is much regret for what we might have done. As time passes and fear becomes habitual, we lose creativity, feel it is too late and lapse into a repetitive, boring life. This situation is alienating for we judge ourselves as rather worthless and feel no one is interested in us—a sure recipe for loneliness.

Fear takes the form of anxiety. The word "anxiety" is derived from the Latin word "angustus" which means "narrow." When our world is narrowed too greatly, we become lonely. One whose world is constantly meaningfully expanding is unlikely to suffer severely from loneliness.

Fear in the form of a serious phobia may be crippling and isolating. For example, one who fears crowds to the point of dread may finally find herself confined to the house, unable to associate with others, unable even to go out, though greatly desiring to do so. Xenophobia (fear of strangers) or fear of germs can separate us from people, leaving us lonely indeed. These kinds of fear have to be treated professionally and the sooner the better; treatment is usually successful.

Paranoia and schizophrenia

One kind of fear not so easily dealt with is paranoia, a general fear someone(s), real or imagined, is "out to get me." It often accompanies schizophrenia or alcoholic syndromes. I saw a man in the throes of paranoia, afraid to stay alone in his room, white as a ghost. He was sure the police were coming for him and that a couple of other residents had "informed" on him. I have never seen such fear registered on a human face. He wanted to remain near me. We had to take him to the hospital. An exaggerated and basically unfounded fear, paranoia is not grounded in reality but very real for the one experiencing it. It is an experience of almost unreachable loneliness in which the person feels alone and unprotected.

Much research is being done on schizophrenia. Although it remains somewhat mysterious, progress is being made. Certain elements of heredity seem to be involved—an abnormality in a gene that appears to be common to many patients—and chemical imbalance, a sort of invasion of the conscious by the unconscious mind because of the disorder. The person who suffers from schizophrenia cannot always distinguish what is happening in reality from what is perceived as happening within the mind.

Schizophrenia is an illness that creates much loneliness for several reasons:

• the person may be out of touch with reality, in a world that others cannot share;

• the person may behave in ways not understood and even threatening to others who, therefore, avoid an encounter;

• the person himself may have to be segregated from loved ones and hospitalized for treatment;

• after discharge, a new sense of alienation often occurs because of the change of surroundings and the attitude of society toward one who has been under psychiatric care;

• the person is conscious of not being able to resume former activities or work and feels marginalized;

• the person may simply not socialize for reasons mentioned in the discussion on paranoia;

• even in hospital the condition of fellow patients makes socialization difficult. At the same time, a safe environment is created and the patient may not be pleased at the prospect of leaving behind a certain group interchange and truth-building.

We have to conclude that the loneliness of one who suffers from serious psychiatric disorders is both mental and physical. We have the image of Ophelia wandering about alone, watched from a distance, and Hamlet, on the other hand, pretending to be mad in order to be able to wander about and eavesdrop! According to the true story of the girl in *I Never Promised You A Rose Garden*,[1] some patients may actually choose to escape the pain of the real world by creating their own world. They then become plagued and haunted by the images in the world they have created. The immense loneliness of this little girl, however, was actually the beginning of her cure. Because she did not want to be alone in the frightening self-made world of images, she chose to leave it and stay with the real world, no matter how painful. She did this only with professional help. Her story provides one clue to the treatment of mental illness.

In order to write not merely from the outside about the loneliness experience of people who have suffered psychiatric illness, I spoke with Walter.

Walter's story

Walter is forty. He now lives alone but keeps contact with friends who helped him, some of whom lived with him in a community house. He smokes heavily. As we sat and chatted in Peter's kitchen, Walter was calm and friendly. I asked him the usual question, more fitting since psychiatry deals very much with images:

"What is your image of loneliness?"

Without hesitation Walter replied, "Being separated from parents and family in the Children's Aid. It's like you're left behind and you'll never catch up."

I asked, "What one word would you use to describe it?"

"Alienation." There was a pause, then Walter went on: "I guess I was always aloof a bit. A loner! Loneliness makes you sad and depressed but you can come out of it: you can call a friend. But alienation—you don't want to."

There was another pause. I waited, not sure if Walter was ready for another question. He resumed:

"I acted up. I would smash a window or something, but then, I was back home and I had domestic trouble—brutality. I hit my mother and the police came. Then I was in the hospital. When you're in the hospital, it's like you're a prisoner. It's all compulsory. [I believe this is less true now, though in cases of violence there is confinement.]

"They said I had schizophrenia. They don't keep you there either and then afterwards you feel more alienation. Paranoia creeps in. You can't do what you want. You can't drive a car. You feel they're after you."

I asked Walter if he is able to work.

"I've worked some jobs. I was with industrial overload jobs. I worked eight weeks with Harvey's but you can only do so many hamburgers, then you can't tolerate it any more. You can't get it together—your mind."

Still, Walter feels grateful that he is not as badly off as many:

"I had more resources. I had some college education. I was smart in school, got a general excellence award in high school. I had a girlfriend in college. I did music, guitar. Sang in a coffee-house. I used to write poetry. And I read a lot.

"But I've sold my guitar—pawned it in England. I had a cousin I visited in England. I also went to Montreal, but I had to go to the hospital there.

"I was in the seminary for a while. People say the church is no help, but it's not true. I don't go to church now, but the people in the church help you. But I couldn't stay in the seminary. My mother had been hospitalized, too, for psychiatric treatment. I had to leave. But I lived in a community—Peter and Laurie and friends have been good to me.

"I'm living alone now. I don't go out much. Now I'm older. I'm forty. I'm satisfied with less—a cigarette and a coke."

I asked Walter: "What do you do to keep occupied?"

"Sleep a lot. I don't do music any more or read much."

"Do you go for walks, get exercise every day?"

"No. Not much. I don't go out much. You get paranoia. You might meet a policeman. I was on the streets for a while. Sometimes I'd go home and mother would give me something."

"Why were you on the streets?"

"You just don't care. You think: 'I can survive.' You don't care. It's more daredevil. I tried suicide—more for daredevil."

"Do you watch TV?"

"No, not much. It's violent. It's like a one-track mind. And you can't get off it. It bothers me so I don't watch."

I turned the conversation now to something more positive and asked Walter:

"What advice would you give someone who has the same sort of troubles you've had?" He answered:

"Pay attention to the social agencies. They help you. They are there to help you. Travel helps if you can do it."

Then Walter added (and I was touched by the compassion and wisdom in his remark):

"I think that singles have the same problem of loneliness as psychiatric people. They have a hard time to have friends, to feel part of society."

Once more I waited and then said:

"Sylvia was saying to me that you were at Laurie's house party last week and there was someone there who was alone and you made the person feel at home and talked with him."

Walter responded:

"I have some resources. I have some education and I know some things."

"Peter says you've come along really well and your friendship with him has grown. Do you think you've weathered the worst?"

"I guess so. I think that's a good way to put it. I think I've weathered the hardest part of my life and I'm a lot quieter now."

I was impressed by Walter's gentle manner of sharing and his willingness to do so. I thanked him and we parted. As Peter walked me to the bus stop, he related his satisfaction with Walter's recovery and his warm affection for him. He was pleased too that Walter had consented to tell us his story.

As is often the case, a hereditary factor is involved in Walter's affliction, an elusive one that doctors are trying to unravel. Also, many persons suffering from mental illness are extremely sensitive as well as talented. This is true of another young man, Norm, who agreed to be included in this book.

Norman's story

I have known Norman for many years, since the early seventies when he came to one of my scripture classes with his friend, John. Norm is a gentle man with a ready smile but eyes that have a touch of sadness—a definite touch. Norm is a poet and a fine one. This chapter contains some poems from his booklet: *Maybe Next Year a Robin*.[2] He is also a good human being who has suffered much mentally.

Norman had sent me a couple of poems for this book, but I wanted more. I was having trouble getting in touch with him. At the moment he lives in a small basement apartment with no telephone. Then one day I met Norm at church and asked to make an appointment to interview him.

"Why not have supper right now?" he invited. I was glad to accept and off we went to a tiny restaurant where I enjoyed time with Norm and recorded some thoughts he shared.

I knew that as a poet Norm deals with images, so the question came naturally:

"What image comes to your mind when I say 'loneliness'?"

He immediately answered:

"Night. Black night."

I pursued:

"What was your worst time?"

"When I was thirteen or fourteen, I had a bad experience of child molesting. I couldn't tell my parents or anyone. But I blamed my parents for never having prepared me or warned me or taught me about life... or what could happen. I didn't know. At that time I became alienated from my father and never got back a good relationship with him. I think he sort of disowned me."

Norman has one sister six years older and one brother six years younger than himself, so he was in a lonely space in the family. The bonding was not close. He went on:

"I kept it all in and eventually it blew, just from all the anxiety. I went hysterical and ended up in jail. Then I got medical help. I was in hospital. But the doctors don't deal with the moral aspects."

At this point I tried to respond with the idea that a person who is in a mentally disturbed state is not free to make a real moral decision and so can't be judged; the doctor deals with the disturbance of the mind. I was sure he had heard all that before but the anguish was still there. I asked, "Did they ever give you a diagnosis of mental illness or was it simply a psychological wound from what happened when you were thirteen?"

He replied, "Oh, yes. They said it's schizophrenia triggered by the event when I was a teenager."

I asked Norm if I could use some of the poems in the book as well as the ones he had sent me. He generously agreed. Of course poems are not autobiographies but they do indicate the poet's ability to penetrate the suffering of the human mind and heart.

Hangover

I've lost great square blocks of memory
On this battlefield
And the fire and smoke is killing, distilling
Once potent brain, now drained, cells
Where I, life's prisoner,
Rot with thought.

Schizoid

My mind halved
Red sharp slices
Of deep thought
Encased, silently
Trapped and mute
Binding to my
Monster hands
And too cruel heart
Beating without sound
Or vibration
In the dark blue nerve
Centre of my mad
And lonely heart.

After visiting a friend in the Clarke Institute of Psychiatry:

In The Clarke 1974

These white walls
Go on forever
Passing me coolly, slowly, lowly
Slides Emma
Big black pupils
Sucking in the walls
So that they breathe and move
To my glance: But I know it is
Only her
I'm just visiting

I see bodies being torn
And bleeding on the floor tiles.
Why can't they see them too?

Life On Uppers

Wading in waters of words
Drowning under an onslaught
Of metaphors
And deadly clique blinks and winks
I feel like rock and wordless sand
Under some dark blue ocean
With floating fly by night
Intellects
Above my quite dead head.

I could not omit the poem that follows for it touches deeply all of the human race in its madness:

Hiroshima B.C.

That time
Nineteen years ago (or yet to come)
They burned the beaten
Melting them like the
Pink wax of a sacrificial
Candle
The stained ball of
The rising sun
I, not yet formed
By God's will and word
Living only on the dreams
Of those who formed me,
I cried in my invisible
Outraged soul
Hanging in as yet unsplit
Atoms
Just a little this side
Of Eden.

Finally, a taste of Norman's religious poetry:

My God
Some thoughts of mine are not really
Mine, but His
He's between my ears and behind my
Heart-protecting ribs
These thoughts sometimes chase
Each mongrel other up and down my
Conscience
And it's only because I'm so good at
Reasoning that I haven't yet become
Fully aware of how much I own that
Hanging man
Who might just as easily have been
Black.

These are the words of the poet with whom I was having supper in the little restaurant. I asked him:

"What helps you most in your loneliest hours?"

He told me:

"Music...like B.B. King, the blues. Also a sense of humour."

Norm is blessed with a great sense of humour: when he mentioned his age it was, "I am almost a year older than Jack Benny" (who is always thirty-nine!). When we began to talk about poetry, Norm asked, "I suppose you want to know, 'What does a poet do in real life?'" His often subtle humour comes across in this poem:

Oscar

Walking one day
With my dog
I passed a starving tramp
Patted him on the head
And fed another biscuit
To my dog, Oscar
Immediately the tramp
Reached out and ate Oscar
In two or three lusty bites

Proving that not all of us
Are as happy as dogs
Or as miserable as some humans.

It was time for the last question:

"What advice would you give someone in your situation?"

Norm's advice is:

"Take time to think before you act, take time. You have your whole life to live. If you find yourself into bad thinking, negative thoughts, turn it around: think of something good."

At about this time, our fortune cookies were brought on a plate. Mine read: "The wise person is one who never gives advice." We both saw the humour in it and laughed.

As we were winding down and preparing to leave, Norman remarked:

"I guess it's a matter of trying to find your home. Everybody is trying to find their home."

He meant this physically, mentally and spiritually, I think. Norm lived in a community house several times but his sensitivity is threatened by outbursts of anger or misunderstandings. These weigh on him too much. He moves out. He is living at this time alone and poorly, working part time. He noted:

"I think outstanding people also experience a lot of loneliness: like someone who isn't just one of the crowd or someone who does something special for which people look up to them or set them apart."

Norman's mental suffering has not estranged him from God. He seems to have a nearness to Jesus that one might envy and is a devout person. He was going off to choir practice at the end of our meeting and seemed eager. It is always a joy to chat with Norm. Still that touch of sadness remains and lingers like a weariness in a line from one of his small poems called "Adieu":

Adieu for one of the Lord's
Thousand year old days....

Another story

Another relatively young man with whom I spoke lives alone in an apartment in the home of a Jewish couple who seem to accept and even appreciate him. He spent five years in a facility for the criminally insane.

"I did five years," he said. "Time is so precious. Now I've got too much time. You know—how do you live so long? I've been out since 1978 but I keep paying for what I did. I try. My heart is open but I'm very, very lonely. And I'm angry that I have to keep paying for what I've done for the rest of my life. I'm a very, very angry person."

Like Walter, this man says he has a difficult time holding down a job. He is also afraid too many questions will be asked or his record looked into when he applies for a job, and that is indeed inhibiting. He added:

"You get sort of paranoid, you know. I want to work but I'm not working now. I do some work around the yard, do the windows, rake leaves, but it's not enough. Now my rent has gone up and I don't know if my cheque is going to cover it. I worry a lot. I also sleep a lot. It's hard to get up in the morning."

There were other dilemmas and contradictions revealing the confusion suffered by this man. He had, in fact, signed off one of our telephone conversations and asked me not to call him, he would call me; but he never called back. Many weeks later, I called to ask if he wanted me to use what he had told me or if he wanted to meet with me or simply drop it. He said I could use it, but not his name and there wasn't much use meeting.

"It's very lonely, you know. I live alone. The couple have gone South now for the winter. I'd like to live with somebody so I wouldn't be alone but, you know, you have to find the right person. I don't want somebody I can't get along with. I want to be free to come and go. I might get someone I can't tolerate.

"I enjoy sitting out on the verandah, come and go as I want. I don't go out much. I go to my sister's. But I don't like too many people.

"It's paradoxical: I just want to be left alone. But I'm lonely....

"I go into a deep shell and get very lonely. But I do the best I can. Well, maybe not the best, but I do what I can.

"My father died. My mother died in 1985. It's never the same. What do you do? The show must go on.

"My older sister phones sometimes. There was trouble over money so we're not too close. My other sister, she's compassionate. I go there twice a week, have dinner...

"I took an overdose but I hope I don't have to go through that again. I just want to keep my life together. I don't want to go over the deep end again. I was in hospital but I had to get out. I couldn't stand it."

I suggested he call his social worker or doctor when he feels himself losing control of his life or getting out of touch with reality. He said:

"They're not there, they're off on holidays or somewhere just when you want them."

But then he admitted that there is always someone there, "like when I took the overdose, there was someone there when I called."

I suggested he go to "Our Place," a drop-in centre for post-psychiatric patients. His response was:

"They all have their own little clique of friends. I feel alone. I have some friends, like Mary Lou... I guess maybe I put all my eggs in one basket. I only see her once in a while.

"I like to watch sports—football, hockey, but then I get tired of that.

"My mother told me before she died to stay here where I am and not to go moving around. She said I moved enough."

I commended the advice, especially in view of the housing shortage, saying he was lucky to have his own place. He could go out, say, to the drop-in where they have meals on Tuesdays, films on Wednesdays, dances on Fridays and entertainment on Saturdays. I suggested that if he went more often he would not feel alone because he would get to know some of the members. I concluded, "Anyway, I think you are doing well and you will manage alright."

The man thanked me for calling and our conversation ended. I was resolved to call him once in a while to break the loneliness. He had said, "You know, when you call someone, you want them to listen. But I get tired of talking. What's the use of talking?"

Still, I felt he was perhaps a little less angry and more settled now than at our last conversation and I hoped he could continue in this state. This man's difficulties are common to so many with psychiatric illnesses, but the suffering is so personal to the one who has it. The nature of the disease makes it difficult for the person to relate to others, even those who have the same sort of loneliness caused by their condition.

Suicide

Suicide is by no means always related to classic mental illnesses. In Japan, for example, suicide is almost expected of one who disgraces the family. For some, it may be a way out or an unwise response, as indicated in the following remarks:

- "They'll be better off without me."
- "I'll be better off."
- "I'm mad and I'll show them. They'll be sorry!"
- "My girl(boy)friend has rejected me."
- "I have an addiction that can't be cured."
- "I've lost all my savings and I'll never be able to regain what I've lost."

Sometimes suicide, especially attempted suicide, is a cry for help. Also, more and more frequently today, suicide is related to drug-taking which may cause temporary insanity, illusions of grandeur and strength, or a "bad trip." Perhaps most often, suicide is a consequence of hopelessness, a hopelessness accompanied by a fearful loneliness as illustrated in this true story told by Sister Gwen:

"Being a stranger in London, I was taking in the sights. Working people were hurrying along Pall Mall to catch the tube home. Down a deserted side-street I saw a sight that froze me in my tracks.

"From the cross-beam of a high iron paling fence, a man was hanging by his neck on a rope. I raced to him. He was alive. I climbed up on the cement foundation and tried to undo the knot tying the rope to the fence. The weight of the man's body was too much. The man was choking out words to me which I couldn't decipher. I tried to pull him onto the ledge but he struck at me and kicked me.

"I yelled 'help' at the top of my lungs and two men emerging from a building came over. All three of us managed to lift the man and loosen the rope while he struggled. The would-be suicide sank to the ledge, gasping, defeated, it seemed, even in this attempt at failure.

"We said things like, 'That was a close one!' and 'Good we found you.' I asked, 'Is there anyone we can call?'

"I repeated the question and had to lean close to hear the answer, 'No one.'

"'Do you have family somewhere that we could contact?'

"'No. All dead.'

"'Is there someone at work....?'

"'Don't work any more... Had to retire two weeks ago,' he coughed.

"The two men looked at each other and the younger one said:

"'I'm going to call a policeman to bring you to a hospital. You need some attention. Can I bring you something to eat? some tea?'

"The man just shook his head wearily. One of the two men picked up the rope, rolled it into a ball and threw it as far as he could over the fence. 'Attempted suicide is a crime,' he whispered, and went off in search of a bobby.

"The two of us sat down on either side of the slumped figure. We asked his name.

"'Harry.'

"'I'm George.'

"'I'm Gwen.'

"Still Harry stared numbly at the ground, but he did not pull back when I took his hand.

"'Where do you live, Harry?'

"'Evan House.'

"George made a face that indicated to me it was no home: hostel of no great reputation.

"'Can we have a friend come by for you, to be with you in the hospital?'

"The same mournful reply came, 'No one.'

"At that moment a short, plump woman came along whose rumpled coat was straining at the buttons. She planted her feet and surveyed the scene.

"'Chills yer bones, don't it, this wevver. No proper summer we've had. You looks as if you could use a fag, mate,' she observed. She rummaged in her baggy pocket and pulled out a somewhat bent cigarette with wisps of tobacco hanging from one end.

"'Ere.'

"Somehow that precious cigarette, foraged from who knows where, penetrated the despair. Harry looked up for the first time as the woman held the cigarette toward him. He reached out and put it between his lips. He slapped at his pockets for a light. George whipped out his own lighter and lit Harry's cigarette. He took a long draw and relaxed a bit.

"'Those hands of yours look as if they've done a lot of work. There's strength in them.'

"'Been workin' steady in the mills since I was eleven. [A glimmer of life!] Never knew my dad [sadness came creeping back].'

"As the younger man came back with a bobby, I felt a silent prayer, 'Dear Lord, let him be compassionate and let this man find a reason to go on living.'

"I don't know what the young man had told the policeman, but he could not have been more understanding. George and I stood up and the policeman sat beside Harry. He pushed his tall hat back and nodded:

"'Under the weather, are you?'

"Harry looked frightened. The bobby proceeded: 'I think you should come to the hospital for a check-up and a bowl of hot soup. I can stop back and see what they say or take you back to your place if you're not up to it. How does that sound?'

"Harry looked at us. I agreed with the bobby's suggestion: 'Sounds good. I think it was not by chance that we found you, Harry.' (Another flicker of life.)

"The bobby helped him up saying, 'Well then, come along.'

"They both nodded and Harry muttered, 'Thanks.'

"'I'd love to come by and see how you're doing,' I added, 'But I fly back to Canada tomorrow.'

"'We'll take good care of him, Miss,' said the bobby as they walked off."

Harry had reasons to feel hopeless and lonely. Too frequently, in our so-called "developed" countries that boast a high standard of living, hopelessness is replaced by meaninglessness which isolates and creates loneliness. Let the poem by Edward Arlington Robinson suffice as a commentary:

Richard Cory

Whenever Richard Cory went down town
We people on the pavement looked at him
He was a gentleman from sole to crown
Clean favoured and imperially slim.

And he was always quietly arrayed,
And he was always human when he talked
But still he fluttered pulses when he said,
"Good morning," and he glittered when he walked.

And he was rich, yes, richer than a king
And admirably schooled in every grace;
In fine, we thought that he was everything
To make us wish that we were in his place.

So on we worked, and waited for the light,
And went without the meat, and cursed the bread;
And Richard Cory, one calm summer night,
Went home and put a bullet through his head.

How different from the French prisoner, "Papillon," who refused to die, refused to let his captors break him, innocent as he was of the crime for which he was imprisoned on Devil's Island! What a daring escape he made in order to live, studying the tides so patiently and finally leaping into the sea to be picked up days later by a passing vessel.

Suicide is, indeed, sometimes the result of real and serious mental disorders and illnesses. "Voices" may strongly urge a person to take such action. These voices speak in a most compelling way, and the patient has difficulty in dismissing them as products of his or her illness and not external realities. On the other hand, the mentally afflicted person may find his or her condition such a torture as to look for an escape in suicide. How often we hear the condition described as "hell."

"Suicide Is Never The Right Answer," reads the headline of one of Ann Landers' columns.[3] Landers is right. Seeking a remedy to health and persevering in it is always preferable, even though it is not easy or simple. No one, absolutely no one, is so lonely or alienated that no other person on earth cares about her, about him. Those closest in kinship, those treating the patient, pastors, friends, acquaintances, people on the end of crisis telephone lines, and future friends not yet met all care. And society really does care about persons being so alienated as to want to die. But often society does not know what is happening; therefore, its care seems to be lacking because it is not expressed. Every suicide is a tear in the fabric of life.

Scriptural consolation

In the cultural setting out of which our Hebrew scriptures came, mental illness was most often identified with "possession." One might conclude, therefore, that little consolation can be found in the scriptures for the mentally afflicted. While there are some instances where possession could actually be the case, the more frequent confusion of mental derangement with possession simply shows the state of medicine at the time. Scientific study of psychological disorders is relatively recent. The symptoms described in some biblical stories are so obviously those of epilepsy, a neurological disease or malfunction now familiar to us, that we have to re-examine and rethink all instances. David, like Hamlet, "feigned" insanity, the one to escape the hands of Achish, king of Gath (1 Samuel 21), the other to be able to snoop and eavesdrop with impunity. They could do this because their societies recognized a certain "innocence" in the behaviour of a mentally unbalanced person and were therefore reluctant to punish the behaviour. Responsibility for one's actions was not seen then as part of the recovery process as it is today.

What does not have to be altered in our consideration of mental illness as seen in the scriptures is the evidence that God, especially in Jesus Christ, has the power and the desire to heal and make whole, when that is for the total good of the person. This must give consolation and hope. Those seeming "demons," the voices caused by an exaggerated disruption of the unconscious into the conscious mind, do not have to control our lives.

I prefer, in any case, to approach the consolation of the scriptures for the mentally afflicted and lonely in terms of the search and struggle for identity in which we are all engaged. I take two scriptural figures: Jacob wrestling with the angel in Genesis 32, and Christ Jesus in Mark 8:27 as well as in his agony in Gethsemane just before his death.

Jacob

Poor Jacob had already been through enough, I should have thought! After all, he had worked for seven years away from home to win the beautiful Rachel and then was cheated by her father who gave him the ugly Leah on the wedding night. Jacob plugged away seven more years, using some ingenuity to increase his possessions, and at last headed home with the two wives, their maids, the cattle, flocks and all. En route, at the ford of Jabbok, he sent all of them ahead across the stream and remained behind. "And Jacob was left alone." Why did he stay behind alone? Something in him seemed to be unresolved. Was it the resentment he carried? Was it fear of returning home to a hostile brother? Was it an inner call to reflect on his life and the new phase he was about to enter?

"And there was one who wrestled with him until daybreak." Jacob was not for giving in or giving up. The one who wrestled finally said, "Let me go." But Jacob persisted; he asked for a blessing. He was required to state his name: "Jacob." But somehow he was no longer the old Jacob. He was given a new name, "Israel," because he had been strong in wrestling with "God" and would also prevail with people in the new life he was about to begin. He did not get an answer when he asked the name of the one he had encountered, yet after the departure of his "assailant," Jacob knew he had indeed established his relationship with God and, in so doing, had established his own identity. "I have seen God in this place and I have survived." But he was left wounded; he limped away. We are told that the people, his people "Israel," held that encounter in reverence in years to come. Jacob's new name, "Israel," has come down in history to this day.

It is not an easy matter, this wrestling with who we are. We only know ourselves in relation to others and to the Other whom we name "God" or Being or Source or Father. In encountering these others we receive wounds and scars. Through these wounds and scars we become the persons we are meant to be.

Jesus

In a centrepiece of Mark's gospel, Jesus asks his disciples, "Who do people say that I am?" (8:27). We might wonder why he asks. Is it not a process of discerning both for Jesus and for the disciples? The disciples offer the various answers they have heard around the country: John the Baptist, Elias, one of the prophets returned. Then Jesus asks very directly, "Who do you say that I am?" Peter answers just as directly, "You are the Christ." His identity is established. But then Jesus says, "Tell no one." He must be named by recognition, not by hearsay. His role cannot be imposed by others, but must be recognized by them.

Then even more surprisingly, Jesus announces that, in his very identity as Messiah, he will have to suffer. He will suffer rejection, which is loneliness indeed, then he will die as a criminal, the loneliest of deaths. Peter, who had identified Jesus correctly, now refuses to accept what must follow. And now, it is not for any "mental disease" but for this rejection of Jesus's very vocation that Jesus calls Peter "Satan"!

Almost immediately we are given the account of the Transfiguration, witnessed by Peter as well as James and John. Again, Jesus' identity is clearly revealed in relationship to others (including God) and to the history of his people, Israel.

I make much of this matter of identity because feeling they are not known is perhaps the loneliest experience humans can have. There is a terrible isolation in it. Perhaps it is at the core of the suffering of the mentally ill in that, in the apparent "unhinging" of the mind, one has a feeling of being unknown even to one's self. At such a time, how important it is that someone "know" us and help us hold together in our confusion and assure us of our identity and well-being. We all need others and others need us in our journey to full identity. We could say it is like needing mirrors to reflect to us what we look like. In the case of God, we can be sure that God knows us most deeply. That is both a consolation and a guarantee. "The very hairs of your head are numbered; therefore, do not fear," Jesus has said. We are known deeply in our very being and not only known but just as deeply loved by God. Though we may feel confused and disintegrated, we are held in our being by God who is life and who cannot fail us. "Underneath are the everlasting arms," says the old poetic version of Deuteronomy 33:27 (Douay-Rheins edition). That is consolation!

That is also why Jesus could, in his agony in the garden of Gethsemane, accept the cup, his cup of suffering. Sweating profusely (a phenomenon well-known to the mentally anguishing), his sweat falling to the ground "like great drops of blood" according to Luke's account, Jesus could hold on to the path of life and of death that was his, stopping in the very midst of his own suffering to heal the severed ear of one of his "enemies" (Luke 22:51). At the heart and centre of Jesus's mental anguish during his passion is a calm, the calm of his own identity that no betrayal, denial, punishment or fear could destroy. Even on the cross, crying out about feeling totally abandoned, Jesus knew to whom he had to cry out and could commit his soul-self—to God, his parent and ours. In our greatest insecurity, we are secure in God. Jesus' suffering and resurrection teach us this. This is why the English mystic, Julian of Norwich, writes so assuringly, "All shall be well, and you yourself shall see that all manner of things shall be well."[4]

It is not only the blind, the deaf and the lame that shall be well but also those who bear the ravages of psychological ills. They too shall be whole and in peace, rising out of agonies to new life.

Lessening loneliness

In seeking to bring help to the psyche that is lonely or ill, one may find that the first step is a medication to ease the pain. This medication may be a temporary means of stabilizing a person so that therapy can take place effectively; it may also be required on a more permanent basis because of the chemical imbalance in the body that prevents the brain and nervous system from functioning normally. Despite some undesirable side effects of drug treatment, it is a mistake to discontinue medications without a doctor's advice: "going off" medication often results in "going off" into further trouble. The same applies to diabetics or persons suffering from any disease or disorder for which medication is a significant treatment.

Numerous therapies

There are numerous therapies, some geared to sick psyches, some more to growth. Freud could perhaps be called the "father of depth psychology," having made a great contribution to psychiatry by studying our complexes and sexual drives. His is not the whole story, of course. Always some methods help one patient more than another. Jungian psychology and therapy stress the integration of the faculties of the psyche: masculine and feminine, light and shadow within. Jung sees this integration as the primary task of all human beings. Glassner's Reality Therapy has proved helpful to many. The importance of keeping in touch with reality and basing health on truth rather than illusion cannot be overstated. One person who has worked for many years with post-psychiatric patients told me:

"I find the best thing is to be myself. That seems to be the most helpful to ground people in reality. If someone tells me that voices told him such and such, I respectfully ask questions to help him arrive at a judgment as to whether these were real or a part of his sickness. If one expresses a seemingly exaggerated anger and agitation over someone or something, I will say: 'I don't feel like that about it. What did they say to make you think this?' I try to dispel illusion with respect but I do not go along with it. Sometimes the persons will then laugh; or I might recommend that they see their doctor or I ask if they are off their medication."

With respect to grounding in reality, John Main, a teacher of meditation, writes:

"The wonder of the experience of prayer [...] is that [...] we awaken to reality—a reality that is everywhere [...]. We must leave the world of illusion and enter the world of reality."[5] This is not to say that a person should always adjust his life to outside reality as if it needed no critique, correction or change. It is not to say that a person ought never to be the "odd man out." But we must know what we are doing, make well-laid choices, and place real foundations under our hopes and dreams.

One therapy, called Logotherapy, addresses the problem of meaninglessness.[6] Its founder, Dr. Viktor Frankl, survived the hell of a Nazi concentration camp where, he tells us, people died because they gave up both their hope and their rations, sinking into meaninglessness. The will to survive and to find meaning in suffering kept Frankl alive. His hope of being reunited with his wife was strong (she, however, did not survive). Being a psychiatrist, Frankl was able to fashion this experience and the will to meaning into therapy. Patients considered hopeless were sent to Dr. Frankl by other doctors. Frankl believes and operates on the belief that deep in the centre of every human being, no matter how mentally ill, is a place of choice.

One woman, for example, had attempted suicide. She had given up living after the untimely death of her brilliant and promising younger son. She was left with her older son who was crippled by polio and needed much care. She experienced a profound anger at the injustice of her fate. Frankl asked her to imagine herself now on her deathbed at the end of her life and to ask herself what she would like to say of herself. In answering the question, the woman found her meaning in life:

"I wished to have children and this wish has been granted to me; one boy died. The other, however, the crippled one, would have been sent to an institution if I had not taken over his care. Though he is crippled and helpless, he is, after all, my boy, and so I have made a fuller life possible for him. I have made a better human being out of my son. [Here she burst into tears, a release of her pent-up anger and the consolation of her discovery.]

"As for myself, I can look back peacefully on my life. For I can say my life was full of meaning and I have tried hard to fulfill it. I have done my best. I have done the best for my son. My life was no failure."

Dr. Frankl notes that the woman had found a meaning "that included even all of her sufferings."[7]

Logotherapy has been especially helpful in treating obsessive compulsive behaviour and fear by the use of "paradoxical intention," which, simply put, means bringing an opposite intention to bear on the one gripping the person.

Personality courses and growth programs

Besides the many therapies for treatment of mental illnesses, there are several personality courses such as the Myers-Briggs and the Enneagram (based on the Sufi analysis of the nine types of people and how they respond to the realities of life). In addition to helping all of us neurotics, these personality profiles promote growth in self-knowledge and, therefore, in maturity and relationships for even the healthiest among us.

After receiving professional medical treatment for mental illness, people can help themselves in many ways. One way is to take part in the GROW program.[8] GROW describes itself as a "voluntary association of people with varying degrees of acknowledged inadequacy and maladjustment who earnestly desire to improve the quality of their lives, and who, through shared learning and mutual help, are finding together the way to mental health or personal maturity." It is inspired by AA, is nondenominational and open to all. GROW has twelve steps, as does AA. Steps 6, 7 and 8 are a sample of the wisdom of GROW:

6. We endured until cured.

7. We took care and control of our bodies.

8. We learned to think by reason rather than by feelings and imagination.

GROW does not replace medical care or treatment by a psychologist or psychiatrist. It is a self-help program to help rehabilitation and growth. It has such helps as the six rules for objective thinking and four stabilizing questions that help in a crisis:

1. What exactly am I troubled about? Be definite.

2. Is it certain, probable or only possible? Be rational.

3. How important is it? Be wise.

4. What shall I do about it? Be practical.

GROW originated in Australia with a man who himself had a very serious mental illness. It reminds its members that loneliness is common to every human being and can never be completely relieved "this side of heaven," but helping one another in small groups is a sure step toward relief. An other step is learning to spend time on one's own thoughtfully, productively, prayerfully, contentedly. It seems to me the word "productively" bears consideration. It does not necessarily mean production with remuneration, in the business sense. Nor does it imply that persons who have had mental illness are forever unproductive. Some outstanding examples prove quite the opposite: William Kurelek, artist, Ezra Pound, poet, Robert Schumann, musician-composer, Walt Disney, cartoonist-moviemaker, Vivian Leigh, actress, Vincent van Gogh, artist, and the founder of GROW.

Another self-help to good mental health is keeping a journal. Writing in our notebook is a way of taking notice of what is happening in our life, of how we are thinking, of the meaning in each event and, perhaps most important, of the patterns in our life. I gave a friend a bound book for Christmas, its pages empty, its cover a mauve-patterned cloth. I suggested she write in at the end of the day only those things for which she was grateful and happy. Weeks later she told me: "I've been following your suggestion and I can't tell you what a difference it has made in my life. I have found many joys I never noticed before."

The journal or notebook is a help to self-knowledge and so to mental health. It is also a sort of companion in our loneliness.

Working in clay, gardening or handling other concrete materials is also a way of dispelling loneliness. After all, we are told God found delight in creation. Such things help us express and ground our feelings which then loosen their grip on us.

Another help is to make a date with a friend, even a new acquaintance, to go and see or do something of interest or share a meal or spend some time at a drop-in or coffee-house. This is not a "romantic" date but simply a recreational way of staying connected with others while leaving them free in the relationship. Mental illness may well mean we are not fitted for the commitment of marriage at least for a period of our life, but it is always realistic and healthful to have good friendships.

GROW recommends permanent daily and weekly routines of life for those with mental instability. These have a firming effect and help ground us in reality.

For the neurotic, refusal to indulge in self-pity, reaching out to others, taking responsibility for setting limits and not over-extending oneself so as to avoid triggering reactions, and scheduling proper recreation are all helpful. The old saying: "Laughter is the best medicine" applies here. Of course what is said here is good for anybody.

For those who suffer more serious conditions of psychosis, obedience to doctors, faithfulness to medication and group participation, and seeking help at the approach of a crisis will help maintain a balanced life.

Above all, let none of us relinquish hope. Many diseases once thought incurable are now controlled and even exterminated—as in the case of smallpox. Work is being done constantly on the mysterious and plaguing sicknesses of the human mind, and much progress has already been made. Every patient who co-operates in his or her own recovery brings success closer. Meanwhile, all of us are called to accept our brothers and sisters afflicted with psychiatric ills in the same way as we are called to accept any other kind of illness. We are learning, together with the sufferers, how to help.

Dying and living with loneliness

I believe that one gets the grace to die. Death seems to be the most natural yet the most unnatural experience possible.

> There is a time to be born
> And a time to die. (Qoheleth 3:2)

In our North American culture, we have, as it were, got used to not dying. We have so many ways of prolonging life and preventing death, so many ways of hiding the truth of it from ourselves with cosmetics or by avoidance, and that despite all the slaughter seen on our television screens. Death is the one thing we surely cannot avoid, even with the expensive possibilities of freezing and revival (cryogenics). In the face of it, we always distance ourselves as if it were not for us, but for someone else. Even those who receive their yearly marking with ashes and hear the words, "Remember that you are dust and will return to dust," somehow avoid the issue. It is not real for us.

As a consequence of death denial, death and dying have become lonelier than ever before. Most people ask strangers to look after their dying ones; this may be a practical necessity as well as an avoidance. Most people will not speak of dying with a dying person or listen to that person's thoughts about it. In effect, the one dying is cut off from the world of the living by this lack of communication and left to inhabit alone the space where he or she is dying. Yet leaving this life is the most important "work" a person will ever do. Among my mother's wise sayings, "As you live so shall you die" makes the connection between dying and living. St. Thomas More, in undertaking to educate his family himself, said it was to be "all to Godward." Thus when they came to die they would do so "full of hope and right merrily." He himself gave an example of dying merrily when he whisked his beard away from the block so that it would not receive the axe since it had not offended!

When we are well and thriving, we are afraid to die. Yet those actually dying seem much less afraid. They pass through the stages of disbelief, anger, bargaining, and coping to acceptance of their position. The space they occupy is lonely because it is difficult to share and impossible to share completely.

I say this from my experience of watching with the dying and from having, in my younger days, experienced grave illness when I confronted the real possibility of death. Once in particular I found myself in a "place" which was quite lonely and which I would describe as "part way over." I had not yet met God but those around me could not enter and seemed very remote. Apparently I had conversations with persons who came to see me but remember nothing at all of these. However, it was not my time to die. I was brought back from that "place" by the anointing of the sick.

Dying may be as lonely for those watching as for the one dying, but with a different kind of loneliness. It would be good for both to speak of the process and share it in some way instead of denying it. I knew a young mother who was dying of cancer but who was able to speak of it with her children and husband.

Together they planned the funeral service as well as the duties each would take on in the family. Her fearlessness and peace were apparent. This may all sound somewhat morbid. Far from it! It was quite realistic and helpful, even consoling, for both the woman and her family. It provided a transition for her own "passover" and for theirs in their continued life together after her death.

A great uncle of mine was a coffin-maker, in the days when coffin-making was an art as well as a service. He had fashioned his own and my aunt's coffins and kept them stored in readiness as they both grew old. I also know a Dominican nun who has her coffin already made in the form of a simple pinewood chest which she now uses both as a storage space and as a bed on which she sleeps. When I visited Thomas Merton's monastery at Gethsemani, Kentucky, and saw the grave where he lies marked by a simple white wooden cross, like all the others, I learned that Trappists do not even have a coffin but are laid in the ground by their brothers, one of whom descends into the grave to receive the body of the brother who has died. Morbid? No. Healthy, realistic and genuine! Were we more prepared to acknowledge our mortality, we would be better able, perhaps, to accompany the dying in a more loving and helpful way that would lessen the loneliness.

My father's death

I watched my father die over a period of ten days. I do not think he was lonely then. He had lived through his loneliness, long days of living alone, thinking, aging, being tested in faith. Now he was pleased that his family had "come home" from the far reaches of this large country. He sometimes awoke and sang, as he loved to do throughout his life, now weakly but contentedly. He still showed concern for his family by questioning, when his meal was brought, "Is there enough for everybody?" It didn't seem right to him that we sat by without sharing his "table." He would pat the bed beside him, meaning, "Come and sit here, very near so that I can touch you." He was sometimes confused. But one day he asked, "What day is this?" "Friday," he was told. Then he said, "One more week." That turned out to be exactly true.

As he grew weaker, becoming a child again as we all do in dying, I watched his strong hands die. I had, in my teens, written a poem for Father's Day entitled, "My Father's Hands." His were a farmer's weathered hands, dependable, work-worthy and tireless. After his death, I wrote this sequel:

My Father's Hands—Part II

Once I wrote a poem
You may have seen
(My friends remember it)
About my father's hands—
I was fifteen.
His hands were big and brown and brawn—
to me, a child, to me so strong.

Now I am forty
And have been through death,
Heard its final breath.

My father's hands were big and strong
But their strength had gone;
They rested
Heavy in mine
And then they died
Surrendered with him quietly
And I cried
Quietly
that hour still a child.
But since—
Well, I have grown some since.

I tell this experience because I feel my father taught me not only how to live but also how to die. In that experience, dying became part of my life as never before. I also understood in that moment of passage that I had but one Father whose life can never end, whose love can never fail.

The death of chronic alcoholics

I have accompanied several of the men from Matt Talbot House in their dying. These chronic alcoholics are not high on the honours list. Yet what most impresses me is the peace I have seen in them, a childlike and humble confidence. They have a true sense that they have no "grounds" for entry into heaven except the goodness and mercy of God. Unfortunately we often do not recognize this truth as these men do and tend to weigh how well we have done in terms of entry, as if we could say, "I've done this and this and this, God, so you owe it to me to let me in." This attitude is also the very cause of our fear. The premises of both presumption and fear are faulty. All of our good works are a response to grace given. Salvation is the gift of God's love and mercy. Realizing this, and realizing that Someone has protected them and cared for them to keep them going against many odds, the men whose dying I have witnessed are peaceful about death. One hears them say, "I'm O.K. I'm ready to go." Or one hears the others say of a buddy who has died, "He's gone into port," or "His troubles are over and he is in peace," or "The Good Man upstairs will let him in."

In conversation with one of the men, dying very patiently and for a long time, I asked him if he needed anything or if anything was troubling him that he wanted settled. He replied, "No, I'm all right. I feel peaceful. I think I lived a pretty good life. I'm not sure what's on the other side. I'll let you know when I get there," he joked. I teased him, "Just don't come in the middle of the night." Volunteers, in the palliative care unit where he was, hovered around and he told me it annoyed him somewhat: "I don't want to tell them to go away but I would rather be left alone. I don't mind being alone. I like quiet." I asked them to leave him in peace except for obvious needs. He died a gentle death.

Another man had a harder time to die, suffering from extreme weakness. I sat with him for some hours on Good Friday, holding his hand. In short phrases for lack of oxygen he said, "I'm glad you came... Glad you came... I'm ready... I want to go." He had no anxieties, only the agony of dying, letting go and waiting in weakness. As I sat on that Good Friday, I felt aware that I was watching the Good Man on the cross.

This peace of the dying was also expressed to me by a friend who spoke with me on the telephone:

"I have just come from visiting a woman in the hospital. She is dying. She could not really speak. It must be very lonely to die. But I felt the deepest peace as I stood by her. Her whole being seemed to be full of peace. Isn't it amazing, such peace!"

It is a lonely thing to die, yet it is the greatest act of humility, the humility of accepting our humanness. As

Paul says in his letter to the Philippians:

> [Jesus] emptied himself and took the form of a slave, being born in the likeness of man. He was known to be of human estate, and it was thus that he humbled himself, obediently accepting even death, death on a cross! Because of this, God highly exalted him.
> (Philippians 2:7-9)

To know that God's Son passed through death in humility and in trust, though in agony and feeling forsaken, to return to God the source of our being is the greatest consolation in the loneliness of dying. It certainly was for Eleanor.

Eleanor's death

Eleanor was a sister and friend in my community who died a premature death from cancer. Sister Eleanor was a very intelligent, witty person who fought valiantly against the disease and never surrendered to it until the end, but kept on serving and counselling others to the extent that she was able. She asked to remain on her mission instead of coming to our infirmary to die, in order to be near her parents and family, and those for whom and with whom she worked in Sacred Heart Parish and in the Archdiocese of Edmonton. She died there on November 30, 1984, while still in her forties.

In the summer of 1983, she knew the cancer was back and I sensed she needed time alone to come to terms with it. I asked her and, having my hunch confirmed, went on my way, shortening my stay by a day. In the ensuing year, I called her from time to time and we exchanged letters. On the Friday before her death, I called. They were having a party in her room! Her voice was strong and she was cheerful. I told her my sister had been diagnosed with cancer. She was shocked. She promised to pray. We talked about how it was for her. She was taking each day as it came, the gift as it was given.

Our community had sent one of our sister nurses to care for Eleanor. Sister Vivian and all who lived Eleanor's dying with her have borne witness that it was a graced time for them. On the Feast of the Transfiguration after El's death, one of them, Sister Pat, wrote the following account which I include here with her kind permission. It reveals the stripping, the human weakness, the loneliness, the desire to die well, and finally, the surrender. It is as a consolation for those who are dying that we place it here:

A thank you to Eleanor now transfigured

"They saw only Jesus"—the Transfiguration over, but its promise remained.

"Now I have only this"—Eleanor's simple but profound statement as she grasped her profession crucifix the night before she died.

"Only Jesus"—that is what life is all about. The lesson of death is how to live.

"One day at a time"—living it every day, Eleanor never needed to say it. She struggled with discouragement and doubt but she never gave up—she always did what she had the strength to do. So she was back at work several hours a day five months before she died, and she saw one of her counsellees two days before she died.

"I don't think I should be this way with it"—she felt betrayed by her anxiety that last night. The reality of life is a part of death. The reality of death is a part of life.

"Lord, I am not worthy to receive you... My God, I renew my vows..."—clenching her crucifix still at five a.m. Did she suspect how close was Transfiguration?

"Pray with me"—almost her last words before the ambulance came.

"Now I have only this"—her fingers tightly clinging, speaking it loudly when lips could no longer form words.

"Pray with me"—her body seemed to cry it in restlessness when we paused between prayers.

"My God, my God, why have you forsaken me?"—she arched her eyebrow as Emmett prayed in her ear, "Jesus, I know you love me." No easy thing—to cling to Jesus only. But her fingers held tight.

"The Lord is my shepherd"—she prayed it often. We voiced it for her as she died, breathing peacefully.

"I shall dwell in the house of the Lord all the days of my life"—her fingers still spoke for her in death, holding fast her crucifix.

"This is my daughter, my beloved"—her face was peaceful with the calm of her last three minutes, her yes to transition from one life to another—to Transfiguration.

Victims of AIDS

These days we are aware, not only of the increased incidence of people dying of cancer, but also of the too numerous cases of persons dying of AIDS (Acquired Immune Deficiency Syndrome). These are mostly men in the prime of life, but there are a number of women and children as well. Because of the dread of infection and because of its association with unaccepted patterns of sexual behaviour, AIDS victims have become the virtual lepers of our time. In times past, lepers were required to dissociate themselves from the community, keep their distance, announce their condition when approached and die alone and unattended. It was a most lonely situation. Now there is treatment for leprosy and knowledge that it is not as infectious as had been thought. But AIDS bears all the marks of leprosy or plague and its victims are skirted and shunned by a large part of society. Added to the immense suffering from the disease itself and the inevitability of death is the immeasurable suffering of isolation and rejection.

One man who died of AIDS in 1987 kept a tape-recorded diary of his last days, his late thoughts. Parts of the diary were published in a daily paper under the title: "The Diary of a Dying Man." They betray the loneliness but also the humanness of those who have AIDS and who are always dying:

"Nov. 10: That's a little cough. I'm not crying. I had my little cry today. I have a little cry now every day.

"Nov. 16: So I have to suffer a little to bring the word out and help a lot of other people. I think that's the only thing that will keep me going in the end.

"Nov. 20: I can't make it to the kitchen for a cup of tea or anything, but there are always people here, thank God, and people helping and taking care of me.

"Nov. 29: I don't know what it would be like, oh God, what it must be like, it must be awful to be alone. That's what I wish people would know. This is the most lonely disease on earth. Even with people around you it's lonely; and to be truly alone feeling this way is everything you've feared your whole life....

"Oh, please, if you know anybody with this dreadful disease be kind, be gentle, be generous because whatever your fears may be, their pain and suffering is much greater. And they're vulnerable.

"Dec. 4: I just don't think I can hang on any more. ... I'm fifty years old. I've had a good life. I've brought happiness, I've brought sadness, I've brought joy, I've been kind to people, I've been generous to people, I've accepted people, I've been selfish to people. And I've made people laugh....

"The days have been terrible. I've thought about all the things one thinks about. Euthanasia. Exit. Going with dignity. And yet something in the human psyche says, 'Hold on.'"[1]

Douglas held on until December 16 when he died at his home in London, England. He did not have the consolation of faith and belief in God although he uses the expression "thank God" in response to the kindness of friends whose care and love overcame their fear of contracting AIDS. Douglas was one of us. He bore witness to the loneliness of dying of AIDS so that other victims might die less lonely. To be assured that in spite of all the mistakes of life one is not abandoned by fellow humans may be the closest some can get to knowing they are not abandoned by God. To help people die, not alone and abandoned, but cared for and loved, was the very inspiration of Mother Teresa's work. That was and is her "something beautiful for God."

The loneliness of those who care for the dying

The loneliness of the dying is also, though in a different way, the loneliness of those close to them who care about them. Those who help people die need someone to support them in their task.

I think of Marg whose husband has Lou Gehrig's disease. The disease is progressing rather quickly. There is an exhaustion in the watching. There is a certain guilt that one is not doing enough, guilt when, at the end of one's own strength, one feels resentful of the patient's demands. There is guilt at one's outbursts of impatience, verbal or not, and guilt at the very thought of placing the loved one in hospital or in someone else's care. There is the loneliness of the day in, day out care, unnoticed and unappreciated by those who go their way to jobs and other activities. Life goes on all around but life has stood still for the one caring for the dying person. Everything else is set aside. And I have not mentioned the grieving that has already begun for the one who is dying, the one with whom a whole lifetime has been lived. In wanting to respond to the loneliness of the dying, one may well look to those accompanying them through this lonely part of the journey.

For someone accompanying a beloved person who is dying, the story of Alice may give wisdom and courage. Alice's husband was dying of throat cancer. He became anxious and wanted her by his side at all times. She felt she could not go out to shop but had others bring supplies in. Weeks passed. Exhaustion set in along with all the "symptoms" mentioned above.

One morning, Alice got up and looked in the mirror. She saw herself worn, pallid, unkempt, as though she too were in a state of dying. She was shocked. Suddenly, like an inspiration from deep within, she received the words, "Alice, this is not your death. This is Tim's death, his own journey. You cannot do this for him. You have a duty to remain healthy, to remain who you are, and in some sense to distance yourself from what is happening to Tim, without guilt or confusion. Live in this truth and you will have the strength and the love to go to the end." It was a graced moment which Alice shared with me, and it enabled her to bear more gently the long last days and the bereavement. We are each given our task and our journey of life and while we go together along the way, we also, each of us, go alone.

In gathering this chapter together, I discovered I had thought a good deal and written more than a few times either, in my journal or in the form of a poem, on the subject of dying. These samples may be some small gift to those experiencing the loneliness of the vocation of dying:

About Walking through the World

.....
Live face to face with everyone and everything
And do not cling
Except to God your source.
For you must die before death comes
And takes you by force.
Before the One who is God have no condition
But only to be a child of true submission
For the world is her warm womb
where she carries you
Until having lived your story
You shall burst forth ready
Into God's glory.

"Cut Grass"

The grass is cut;
...
This at least
Let me glean from the grasses—
Sweet scent from me
Spring when my Mower passes.

One of Us Came Back

Death, what are you, death,
And where?
Long have you threatened us with cold
Despair.
Now you are uncovered,
Sting of death!
One of us came back
And told the truth.
Yes, one of us came back
From death
And now you are exposed.
There is no space, no tunnel dark,
No Styx, no void.
These are the body things
We fear.
Body stays: its rest
Is here.
We awake in light
And know
All we have ever known
And more:
The Presence and the ones we knew
Before;
A consciousness at once
Complete
And knowledge full of joy,
No, death,
Your power is not mortality,
for Life
Awaits and breaks upon that sea
Of all vitality.
   (written on the occasion of the death
  of a young friend, Sister JoAnn Brdecka)

The Fooling of Death (Dec. 8, 1981)

One who had come to the end
Of the way of wending

In the world
Waited
With bated breath
For death to come
But death was dazed
Amazed:
It came as no surprise
Meeting the eyes
Of a Son
The one
Who had cheated
Defeated death
Put it beneath
His feet.
No darkness
No starkness
Marked that passing
To everlasting
Surpassing joy
Seeing the boy
Who had his birth
From her earth.
There was heard
The sound of song
From the expectant throng
Swelling like the dawn:
"Hail, Mary!"
And she
Again replying:
"The Almighty
Has done great things for me"

When can I enter and see the face of God!
...
How I would lead the rejoicing crowd
Into the house of God
Amid the cries of gladness and thanksgiving
The throng wild with joy.

(Psalm 42)
(This is on the dying of Mary,
written on her feast day.)

Chronically ill

We are all called upon to live until we die. This is not trite. Especially for those who are chronically ill, it is a serious mission. I use the word "mission" purposefully. In the new sacrament of the Anointing of the Sick, there is a sense of the sick, particularly the chronically suffering, having a real mission in the Church and world. If we have learned one thing from the example of Jesus Christ, it is surely that suffering is redemptive... or can be. But it can also be very lonely. We can hardly blame those who have suffered long for complaining, "Why doesn't God come for me?" or "How long, O Lord?" especially when others their age have "gone home." But many of these chronically ill persons are determined to live until they die. They have a sense that, no matter the conditions, life is very precious. One who became ill, not from the ravages of age, said: "I never knew until now how precious life is. Live it to the full while you have it. Every year, every month, every hour is precious."

Many of the chronically ill are tempted to think that they are useless, a burden to others, without a "role." As we know, persons out of circulation because of sickness are often shelved or feel so. Others cannot find time to visit on a regular basis, or find the conversation very limited. However, many sick people are remarkably alive and able to reach out in the midst of their illness. One such person is Sister Marie whom I met while in Pembroke, Ontario. Afflicted with porphyria, she cannot bear much light and is confined to her room. Because the disease causes her to swell, she must avoid salt; she is nearly blind from this disease and suffers excruciating headaches and prolonged blackouts. But what a spirit!

I asked Sister Marie what image comes to her mind when I mention loneliness. She answered:

"Well, I was a violin player for thirty-three years and I get very lonely when I am not able to play any more. This is the worst."

She repeated this in her letter to me recently. This cheerful woman loved to play and also to dance. She laughs that she did not enter the convent "until she had danced enough." When I asked what was her worst time, she came back with:

"My worst time is not that bad because with my work and my closeness to God, God is very good to me. And I am so grateful for my good community leaving me my freedom in my work."

What is that work? Sister Marie, unable to continue in the active field of caring for the aged, took addiction counselling so that she could "work" right in her sickroom. She has a telephone, soundproofing, and a stream of alcoholic men and women coming to her door:

"I tell them they have to be sober four weeks and have an AA sponsor. I don't talk to cobwebs."

As you may discern, Sister Marie is not a pushover. She is tough with her clients but she also understands them:

"My disease has helped me to understand alcoholics. Sometimes I say to them, 'You have a disease and I have a disease. Mine is incurable. Would you like to trade?'"

She tells how she sneaked into the pickle jar and gorged herself with the result that she was "salted" and became extremely ill, like the alcoholic who cannot stop before the bottle is empty. But she also says those who come for help are a help for her. How else could she bear her pain except for all of them. Her prayer, too, is for them and sometimes her pain is her prayer.

This woman has found her outreach in the midst of her great limitations. Fortunately, as she says, "I'm not a shy person: when God gave out shyness, zoom! it went right over my head." This woman knows the pain of loneliness and knows that the fear of it is often a cause of alcoholism. Her treatment combines common sense with much love. Of her apostolate, Sister Marie says: "God isn't asking me to do the impossible. He'll do that: I just do the possible." And she is doing that with wonderful effect. She has reached hundreds, including persons from other countries, although she never leaves her room.

Undoubtedly, the chronically ill must spend many hours alone and will experience loneliness and limitation. To know that they have a mission in all this can be a way out of that loneliness, or a meaning for it.

Being chronically ill or dying is not easy. Jesus wept over the deaths of his friends and he wept over his own death. We need not be ashamed of weeping. Jesus showed a compassionate heart also for the sick, especially for those who had lingered a long time: the woman bent over for eighteen years, the man who lay paralyzed for thirty-eight years hoping to get into the water when it stirred but always being left behind, the lepers, the blind from their birth. Still, he did not cure them all, not all the lepers, not all the blind, not all the paralyzed. As Sister Marie says, she has come to regard her sickness as a mysterious blessing. Would she indeed have reached so many and ministered to them had she not had to search out her new mission in chronic illness?

Scriptural consolation

The one truth that the sick as well as the dying can cling to is that they are never alone. Their shepherd, who has passed through death, is with them in the darkest valleys.

Travelling in the south of British Columbia past Creston, perched on the mountainside, I grasped the image of "the valley of darkness" in Psalm 122, the Good Shepherd psalm. In the afternoon, the sun was shining on the snowy mountaintops, a beauteous and uplifting sight, while the wooded valleys were very dark, almost forbidding. On mountaintop or deep valley, the Shepherd knows our route and is always leading us to the place of water and refreshment. Those not able to walk he carries. "There is nothing they shall lack."

The psalms are good prayers for us to pray or hear prayed for us in our joy and in our distress. Jesus, as he was dying, used the words of Psalm 30 (31): "Father, into your hands I commend my spirit." Psalm 16 says:

> And so my heart rejoices, my soul is glad;
> even my body shall rest in safety.
> For you will not leave my soul among the dead,
> nor let your beloved know decay.

Let the ill and the dying know that they are, in the words of St. Paul, "a spectacle to angels and to humans," their fellow travellers, to those who have gone before, to those who remain and to those who will come after, to whom they give their witness until the end, living until they die and enter life anew. Do we not cry out at the liturgy of eucharist, the memorial of Christ's death and resurrection:

> Dying, you destroyed our death.
> Rising, you restored our life.
> Lord Jesus, come in glory!

Lessening loneliness

- For the sick: allow others to minister to you, to care for you. It is often a grace for both sick and visitor or attendant to communicate.

- Do all you can to get well.

- When the sickness is chronic or long, be mindful that it is your "mission" or vocation at this time, and that it is beneficial if borne well.

- Reach out to others as you can, especially others suffering as you do.

- When too ill to pray, don't worry. Let your body pray and cry to God without words.

- You are part of a mystery called "the paschal mystery": the death and resurrection of Jesus Christ who is the pattern of our lives. Nothing is wasted. You can still be a witness to many through your love.

- For those in the dying process: it would be helpful to know that there are stages one goes through, from disbelief, through anger to acceptance and peace. These are normal. A chaplain, a friend or books (see those by Dr. Kübler-Ross) may help you to go through these stages more fruitfully.

• Especially do not be afraid to speak of your journey. Every person will take such a journey. Your loved ones can share it with you. But they may not wish to open the topic. Be simple and say what is going on. It will help everyone.

• Write, draw, express, communicate.

• These times of seeming passivity and loneliness are a moment of letting God's ways be done. You are not going alone. God in Jesus Christ has revealed that death is not the last word but life. Jesus has gone before you and goes with you at every step. Pray for great trust in him. You will be graced for the journey of sickness and of dying.

Sentenced to loneliness

Having walked through a number of prison gates and penitentiary halls, I have to say that I think there is no place less private or more lonely than a prison. On the one hand, the prisoner's individuality is not respected. He or she is one of the "prison population," an "inmate." On the other hand, the prisoner is so alone, so removed from all loved ones, so cut off from the familiar as to be the image of loneliness.

What is worse, there is, despite cliques and a certain camaraderie, no one whom the prisoner feels he or she can trust or wants to trust. This is partly because, by the very fact of their imprisonment, these individuals have shown themselves untrustworthy in some way. It is partly because there is such a high level of fear despite the exterior toughness and bravado. It is partly because no prisoner wants to be persecuted by fellow prisoners for positively co-operating with staff who might be really caring and helpful. It is partly because not all staff are worthy of trust. These are the harsh facts.

When I first began to take part in a prison program at Warkworth Penitentiary, an all-male, medium security facility, I felt that the men, whose average age was twenty-two, would not relate to me because I was "a nun." To my great surprise, I was approached by several persons on various occasions, in the time we designated for "one-to-one." The conversations followed a line similar to this:

"You're a nun, eh?"
"Well, yes. I'm a sister."
"Uh...uh...you don't get married, eh?"
"No, but I live in a community with other sisters."
"Uh...you take some vow or something?"
"Yes."
"Like...uh...you don't have sex?"

"That's right. We take what we call a vow of chastity to live without a husband or children because of Jesus Christ to whom we give our love. And we love all people and especially children whom we teach and care for."

"You mean you can really live like that...like...without sex?"

"Yes, with God's help and for love of God. Of course, sometimes it's hard. Sometimes we'd like a husband and children and all that, but just like someone who is married, we vow to be faithful to this way of life."

"It's really possible?"

"Yes, it's really possible."

There is a pause. What is really behind this conversation? Is it curiosity? Is it small talk? No. It is hope. What comes next is:

"Maybe my ol' lady [my girlfriend, my wife] will be able to hang in there and wait for me. I can't expect her to wait. I got myself in here for [...] years and I wouldn't blame her if she got some other guy. Geez, I hope not. Maybe it's possible. Maybe I'm gonna tell her about you. But I wish I could see her oftener. It's hard when you can't even talk to her. I guess it's lonely for her too."

What is behind these repeated conversations about my being a nun with a vow of chastity is that these men, especially the ones with long term sentences (in federal prisons, two years and over), are very lonely people. They are lonely for their families, especially their wives, and they live with the gnawing fear and anxiety that their loved ones will not be waiting for them when they finally get out. As their stay in prison lengthens, usually visits become less frequent, a fact that is encouraged by the building of penitentiaries far from the centres of population and with inadequate access by public transportation. The situation results in alienation of the worst kind for people who are already alienated from society in general either because of the long imprisonment or because of the anger and resentment which drove them to criminal behaviour.

The seeming hardness of people in prison hides the fears and the tears. For some, the loneliness has been unacknowledged and suppressed and will become further alienation from humanity, further crime even. All of this is reinforced by the fact that society, all of us, finds it very difficult to allow offenders to be trusted or to become "normal" members of the community. It is a classic case of the chicken and the egg: we cannot trust them because they have criminally offended our society; yet they can never be rehabilitated (live in society) unless we trust them as neighbours or fellow workers or employees.

Intimacy, connectedness and types of loneliness

Richard Gilmartin, psychologist, in a lecture about loneliness, laid out the needs we humans have with respect to intimacy, connectedness and types of loneliness. It seems to me these are particularly important as they apply to those who are imprisoned, and so I sketch them out here. Humans need intimacy of several kinds:

- emotional intimacy of shared feelings;
- intellectual intimacy of shared ideas;
- aesthetic intimacy of shared creativity;
- recreational intimacy of shared effortless relaxation;
- crisis intimacy of shared pain;

- spiritual intimacy of inner values and growth.

No one person can be expected to fulfill all of these kinds of intimacy to the fullest and so we need many shared relationships with many people. Too often, people use sex to replace intimacy and to escape loneliness.

The kinds of connectedness we all need for fullness of life, health and coping with loneliness are:

- cosmic connectedness: sensing that we are at one with God and the universe;
- cultural connectedness: sensing our bondedness with origins, our belonging;
- social connectedness: being accepted by a community of friends, family, associates;
- interpersonal connectedness: experiencing one-to-one relationships of depth and understanding.

To the degree that one or other of these is lacking, the others may compensate.

Finally, the types of loneliness are chiefly:

- abandonment by or loss of a significant person;
- lack of a person or persons for whom we feel significant;
- need of parents or parenting now (at any stage).

In checking over these lists, it becomes evident that the life of the imprisoned person lacks all or most components. The intimacies are cut off or curtailed physically, environmentally and personally (since it is difficult to have trusting and therefore intimate relationships among the incarcerated or with staff). The connections are broken or never existed. Even the language used in prisons reveals the disconnectedness: "on the outside," "out there," "in here." It is possible but not probable that a person in prison can find or build the intimacies and connections listed by Gilmartin. It is much more likely that connections will be broken rather than built. The probabilities leave the imprisoned wide open to the three kinds of loneliness listed.

Those in prison are removed from those for whom they feel they have some significance, and those who are significant for them are walled out. Add to this situation the sad fact that many of those who have committed crimes for which they are sentenced to prolonged prison terms have lacked good parental bonds and still suffer that lack all through adulthood. All the conditions for extreme loneliness are practically guaranteed.

It is possible, if difficult, for persons to endure and survive prison and even to find and build their lives by establishing themselves in groups teaching and learning life skills. I have personally known some who responded, as with a great hunger and thirst, to the personal growth programs we, as a Youth Corps, shared with the men and women in prisons over long periods of time. The building of trust, values, and connections "on the outside" enabled some to speak their hearts, ask questions, reflect and make positive decisions and choices about their lives. They began to be integrated first within themselves and then with the group and, finally, with society "out there" to which they would one day return.

One person stands out in my mind, Brian, a "lifer," who was a gentle person and came regularly to our group. The situation in which he committed his crime might well have led anyone to a life sentence; this is not to excuse him. Brian experienced conversion in the deepest sense and in ways which affected every facet of his life. He eventually earned parole and married the daughter of one of our group who had developed a real and lasting relationship with him. He became reconnected.

But disconnectedness and extreme loneliness are the norm for most of the imprisoned. While it is true that there are opportunities in prison for updating one's education or learning a trade, the person in prison either sees no future in it or, more often, like the disturbed child in the classroom, is simply unable to apply him or herself to books or learning. Personal anxiety, misery or habits make it next to impossible to perceive the value of such efforts. "Nobody out there will give me a job anyway once they find out I've got a record."

Added to the general disconnectedness of life in prison is the practice of solitary confinement. Those in prison call it "the hole." It is the ultimate method of subjugation and of breaking the spirit. It is also used in the form of "protective custody" for persons found guilty of sex offences, in particular child molesting. There is a pecking order even among the punished and the sex offender is at the bottom of the list. He is not safe from fellow residents and would be the first victim of violence within the walls. Protective custody is the solution used. But it takes a strong sense of self and of personal identity, relatedness and purpose to be able to spend long hours, days, even months, alone. The story is told that when St. Thomas More was in solitary, deprived of his books as additional punishment, his hair turned white overnight.

Example of victory over prison alienation and loneliness

Even in these circumstances, one with purpose and connectedness and a good sense of self can make, of the unbearable loneliness of the prison, a place of meaning and of life. A friend and well-known war resister, James Douglass, has spent periods of time incarcerated for civil disobedience at the Trident nuclear submarine base at Bangor, Washington. His purpose as a peace activist is very strong. He bears witness to the fact that prison has become for him his monastic cell, his desert of contemplation, his garret for writing. He also makes his time in prison an occasion of creating some community and humanizing prison life. We recall such other exceptional prisoners as the Birdman of Alcatraz and the Frenchman, Papillon, who, because he was innocent of the crime for which he had been sentenced to life on Devil's Island, was absolutely determined not to be broken and to escape. He finally did, by means of his ingenuity and courage; he jumped the high cliff with a net of coconuts and floated out to sea on a current. He was given Venezuelan citizenship for the very stature of his human spirit.

Other examples of victory over alienation and loneliness of the prison are the political prisoners who have survived untold ordeals of interrogation, torture and solitary confinement. The names of Jacobo Timerman[1] (Argentina), Sheila Cassidy[2] (Chile), Anatoly Scharansky (USSR), and others come to mind, but they are many, too many. There are also the "disappeared," a modern phenomenon; it is as if, the smarter and more "civilized" we become, the more refined our cruelty. The disappeared are swept away from sight or contact, often without warning, and usually are not seen alive again. The loneliness of the disappeared is unimaginable and nearly equalled by that of their families and loved ones who wait hoping for some word. The disappeared are the prisoners of what I call "death row anonymous."

The loneliness of death row

Then there is death row itself, still in existence, not yet a thing of history. Death row is a lonely place indeed, lonely with the loneliness of imprisonment and lonely with the loneliness of the dying. To write of it seems shallow and patronizingly pitiful. Only the experience itself would be authentic in the telling. The person condemned to die is virtually labelled unfit to live as a member of the human race. In that judgment more than one innocent man has died. Whatever the guilt of any individual, to be assigned the label "not human" is a lonely thing. The long, long walk to the gallows of whatever kind, knowing that some fellow human is about to dutifully administer death, no matter your inner state, with no future possibilities, must be the ultimate alienation. Bad enough for a human to be condemned by impartial disease, targeted by war, victim of brutal accident; in these cases, at least, there is recognition, compassion, heroism, shock and regret that a human has to die. But to walk to the death chamber largely unmourned is a prospect lonely beyond words, with an aloneness that cannot be cured. Blessings on those who stand by such a one.

If we look at the three crosses on the Calvary on Good Friday, we see three men condemned to die. For two of them, we know of no family or friends who were present.

For the third, despite the faithful presence of a broken-hearted mother, some devoted women friends and one, only one, of his near companions, the loneliness was hardly less. It was so great that he cried out in a loud voice: "My God, my God, why have you abandoned me?" It was his God and his Father who seemed to leave him there alone to die. That is loneliness indeed.

The importance of establishing connectedness

These are some of the degrees of loneliness that are suffered by the imprisoned. In the context of connectedness as opposed to loneliness, one can see the importance of groups of prison visitors such as Springboard and the John Howard Society whose members can also help with the transition from prison back to society. Other groups have arranged transportation for relatives to visit their imprisoned loved ones on a regular basis and at affordable cost. Others have provided houses of hospitality where visitors may stay for a few days if they have come a long distance to visit prisoners, members of their family.

The prisoner, even the so-called hardened criminal, is not immune to the need for human relationships and connectedness. Often, too, the relatedness to other people is the measure and means of their relatedness to God, as is true of all people. It is often difficult for people rejected by society not to feel rejected by God also. That is loneliness. With the growth of trust and friendship between persons in prison and others who come to them comes a re-connectedness to God, a sense of acceptance and forgiveness.

I was deeply impressed in this regard by the prayer composed sentence by sentence by a group of men and members of our group who went regularly with a challenging program of values input and fellow-ship, always with an element of prayer. It was Thanksgiving Day and this is the prayer that came from their hearts:

> Thank You for the gift of people.
> People who shine with courage.

People who help me to change,
Who stand by me while I'm growing
Out of my old self into my new self.

Thank You for people who help me to hear
When I am deaf, to see when I am blind,
Who help me to change my mind

Thank You that people too can change,
Can forgive and forget and receive me again,
And trust me when I've been away
And I've come back.

Thank You for children who love life
And show us that life is good, beautiful, and fun,
Who in their growing pains come to us
With confidence, calling forth our caring
And our loving.

Thank You for those who share with me
And receive and respect my sharing,
Who didn't leave me alone when I cried,
"Leave me alone!"

Thank You God for caring so much
That You sent Your Son Jesus to bring me
On my journey home.

Thank You for being more father and mother to me
Than my own parents.

I did not compose this prayer; I only write it down. Parts of it are in the handwriting of men in the group. If it looks like a poem and sounds like a poem, maybe it is a poem and maybe there are poets in prison who suffer the loneliness of the artist as well as the loneliness of the prisoner.

It follows that society, that is, all of us, and especially those of us related to or acquainted with persons incarcerated, have a real responsibility to keep sending signs of remembrance and connectedness into the prison life, through visit, letter, card, package, telephone or just some meaningful symbol.

The song, "Tie a Yellow Ribbon Round the Old Oak Tree" became extremely popular a few years ago. The song expresses feelings, not only of the prisoner about to be discharged, but of any one of us in many a situation; hence its popular appeal. The singer has "done my time" and writes to test the waters of his reception. In brief, the message is: If you want me back, give me a sign: tie a yellow ribbon.... He acknowledges, "I'm really still imprisoned" until those he hopes will accept him give him the "sign." With great relief we hear the last verse:

"And I can't believe I see
A hundred yellow ribbons round that old oak tree."

What such a sign is saying is: I have faith in you that your life can begin anew. Every person "doing time" needs to see a yellow ribbon.

Scriptural consolation

In the scriptures, there are prisons, images of slavery as well as a physical reality. In the Hebrew scriptures, prison seems to be less for the wrongdoer than for the one who shakes the system or threatens the power structure; one thinks of Joseph and of Daniel. Then there is John the Baptist who stands between the two Testaments. He must have lingered lonely in the Herod's dungeon, for he sent messengers to Christ seeking confirmation that he was indeed the expected one, the Messiah. John must have thought, "What if this is all for nothing. Could I have been mistaken?" As we know, John did not come out alive. His witness, nonetheless, is still reverberating down the centuries.

And then there was Jesus. He too was in prison. Neither did he get out of it alive. He is still in prison, for he said: "When I was in prison, you visited me" (Matthew 25), identifying himself with every prisoner. Jesus' apostles, too, eventually found themselves imprisoned for "obeying God rather than men" (Acts 4:19). The escape of Paul and his companions and the release of Peter seem to have been not only literal events but symbols of the return to the community as the end of alienation, disconnectedness and loneliness (Acts 12 and 16).

Lessening loneliness

• Avoid "out there" and "in here." You are still part of society, part of the human race. You affect the population by your presence.

• Noble persons have been in prison. Imprisoned persons have become noble (e.g., Birdman of Alcatraz, St. Maria Goretti's murderer).

• Take advantage of what is offered: learn a trade, upgrade your education, make use of time.

• Learn to pray. The chaplain is a friend. So is God.

• If psychological help is offered, take advantage for your growth.

• Stay with reality. Imagination may make you more lonely unless you are positive and practical in its use. It can multiply your troubles and prevent you from seeing and using what is in front of you.

• Seek out others who are serious about changing for a better life. Help one another.

• Write. Keep a journal or diary of feelings, events, changes you see. You do not have to be a "writer" to do this. Keep your own "record."

• Read. Develop the habit. Books are friends. If you have trouble with reading, get help with upgrading. Choose constructive books such as biographies.

• Learn to be contentedly alone. Remember others have chosen solitude and still others endured it. You are a good person who may have done something wrong. Your story does not end here.

• Find a hobby and do physical exercise. Both dispel loneliness.

- You still have a choice in every circumstance, even if it is a choice of attitude only. Relate to others but make your own choices.

- Friends and relatives: keep in touch and help persons in prison stay connected with society. Write, visit, send some sign of remembrance. Feelings of isolation can be dehumanizing and cause great loneliness. If you can, be part of a program going into jails and prisons.

The loneliness of separation

The word "separation" must be the loneliest word in our language. It bears the sense of division, physical rending, and the breaking of the human heart. Whether separation results from the necessary absence of one dearly loved, whether it is through death or failed relationship, the word connotes an idea and a feeling heavy with pain. The name of that pain is loneliness.

This chapter tells stories of separation loneliness experienced by men and women like ourselves. These have passed through their separation and begun to live again by positive choice, though not without scars.

Separation from children

The first account tells of the excruciating loss of a child. A school friend of mine failed to send the usual Christmas card. But at that same Christmastide, I learned from another classmate of the loss Lynda and her family had suffered. I sent Lynda a note and received a reply which read:

"This Christmas we sent very few cards mainly because I just couldn't go on explaining with each one why a name was missing. Yes, we gave [...] our darling Amy back to her Father last May. [...] She died while Jack and I were on a three-day weekend away together. It was a shock on our arrival home from which we have not yet recovered and I wonder if we ever will."

Even as I rewrite Lynda's words I recall the words of Elie Wiesel, Nobel Laureate, in *A Beggar in Jerusalem*:

"Anguish grips me, as though I were about to meet something as absolute, as decisive, as pure as the death of a child at dawn."[1]

Amy's death was one of those sudden and mysterious illnesses that can seize a child. And though nothing could have been done, the trauma to parents and to family members caring for the children that weekend was indescribable. A few years have passed but when recently I wrote to Lynda and Jack requesting to use their story and asking them to write some thoughts that would help and console others who experience the terrible loneliness of bereaved parents, I did so realizing that I was asking my friends to remember their pain. I did it because I believe they took positive steps to help themselves to bear that pain and to go on with life, and because their encouragement would be invaluable to others. I was shocked to learn from them that seven out of ten marriages break up after the loss of a child. Why? Because a gulf seems to yawn between the two spouses grieving in two different ways not understood by each other. A loneliness grows in each because of this widening gulf.

Fortunately for these two beautiful persons, Lynda and Jack, they realized that something was happening to their good marriage: they knew they needed help. Fortunately, too, there was someone to direct them to Bereaved Families of Ontario.[2] Lynda writes:

"Hopefully this will be of some use. While my desire to make a contribution is sincere, the intensity of the feelings makes expression difficult.

"While I know that loneliness shows itself in different ways to different people, for me it never meant being alone, that is, by myself. Rather it expressed itself in alienation, a lack of communication, isolation. Never was this manifested so strongly as after Amy's death. No one—parents, siblings, friends—was able to leap that chasm which separated them from me. In my brokenness I was unable to reach out. This inability to touch each other resulted in a previously unknown and terrible awkwardness. But the truly devastating aloneness was in our marriage.

"Jack and I had read of the high percentage of marriage breakdown following the death of a child, so we thought we were equipped to handle the time. But once again we were constantly faced with the awareness that heart acceptance does not live in the same neighbourhood as intellectual awareness.

"It may sound trite and overworked, but the reality was that we had become like strangers to each other. Openness was replaced with defensiveness, energy with a great weariness, hope with cynicism. The present longed for the past and the future stretched bleakly ahead. Playfulness and spontaneity became formal and stilted rituals, and intimacy, while longed for, exacted a giving which was too demanding for wounded souls. Confrontation too was exhausting, so we retreated to our own dark space."

I do not know when I have read such an accurate description of almost complete and total loneliness. Lynda continues:

"Months after languishing in that netherworld, I panicked that Amy's death was resulting in the death of our family as we knew it. Together Jack and I went to a bereavement counsellor at Bereaved Families of Ontario. She re-assured us that what seemed to be a marriage problem was, in fact, a grief problem.

"The door was opened, the light entered and truly I felt resurrected. Still lonely! but knowing once again that I was alive and with all probability would survive, and our marriage would too."

Lynda, writing for both herself and her "very private" husband, Jack, ended the above saying it was "all I am able to give at this time." But some weeks later she sent me a letter which bore some important additions or reflections. She refers to the introduction to her "saga" which I had sent her to read:

"Your words of men and women like ourselves who have begun to live again, by 'positive choice,' struck a chord which I had originally wanted to address. The mystery of Amy's death remains that unexplained 'Why?' What is almost equally puzzling, however, is the 'presence' of something that connects and binds us to the mothers and fathers of all lost children.

"During those awful final moments at the graveside, I remember thinking and saying to myself: 'Other mothers have done this.' The horror of all children's deaths washed over me, yet I did not feel abandoned—that came later. On many occasions when I was too tired, too depressed, too alone to make that positive choice, I honestly believe that such a 'body' made the 'yes' for me.

"With the knowledge of any child's death since Amy's, that realization is reinforced as I unite myself with those parents and try to will them through their loss. Friend or stranger, acquaintance or unknown, it doesn't seem to matter.

"Painful, yes. But somehow cleansing, too; to believe that one can silently offer consolation and the knowledge that it can be survived.

"If this added insight is useful, it's yours to use. Jack and I thank you for accepting our contribution."

It is I who must thank Jack and Lynda. This "added insight" seemed to me to be truly a leap from isolation of loneliness to the experience of the Communion of Saints.

Saints are ordinary women and men who have come through the great trial of life in a spirit such as Lynda and Jack have shown. As I have shared their loss more deeply than they know, so I have reverenced them in their saga.

Other poignant forms of separation of parent and child occur when, for example, a child is given over for fostering or adoption by others. No one but a parent can possibly know the experience of the long loneliness of separation. The rest of us can only feebly imagine it.

Many a single parent has a story to tell of the loneliness of "being left." One of these is Gloria. When I told her of this book, she began to tell me of her own life with her daughter in a large apartment complex in a large city.

"My image of loneliness is standing on the balcony looking out and wondering how one could be so lonely living among so many people. It seemed unfair. It wasn't so bad until the day Jennifer started school. Before that, I stayed home and looked after her but suddenly she was gone with others and I was alone. I was terribly lonely. I was so lonely that I did things I never should have done to get away from that loneliness.

"Later, I started going to AA meetings for the fellowship—I still go. I realized it was also a lack of social skills and my inability to approach people. I was always a loner that way. I was a very well-behaved child who was praised for being quiet. I'll never forget the first time I was able to go into a meeting by myself, walk in and sit down on my own. I was so proud of myself—at thirty-five years old, for gosh sakes!

"Now I know a lot of loneliness is the attitude to oneself. When Jennifer started school, it was the first time in my life I was ever alone and I was terrified. Now I can enjoy being alone. But still I sometimes think of the time when Jennifer will be gone and it worries me some, but I'm more mature now. I worry about Jennifer, too, being an only child. It's hard being an only child. If something happened to either one of us, it would be awful."

Gloria and Jennifer are good friends growing up together, as it were, and facing these fears together.

Death of a spouse

Another kind of separation, the separation of spouses, companions of a lifetime, brought about by death, is a loneliness that must, inevitably, come to one or other of the two except in rare cases when both die together, as in an accident. While bereavement and grief are not identical with loneliness, they contain it or are followed by it. Every widow, every widower knows.

Nearly ten years ago where I was working at Shoppers' Drop-In on Yonge Street in Toronto, Dora walked in. She was a distinguished-looking woman, tall, quite slim, impeccably dressed, gentle in manner, her face drawn and grave. It was the first of many visits Dora would make to our drop-in. As her story unfolded, we learned that she had been fairly recently widowed. Only much later would I come to know what that first visit meant. I invited Dora to come back and share with me for this book because I knew she had come through her own loneliness in such a way as to be able to help many other bereaved spouses. But let Dora tell her own story:

"I had a very happy marriage. We had no children but we had just had eleven wonderful years in the Bahamas. Because of the political situation there we returned to Canada and bought a small flower business in Toronto. We were so happy with it and pleased to be back in our homeland with my mother and extended family nearby.

"Then one day, Bronek dropped in the flower shop and died right there. It was totally unexpected, totally unbelievable."

She recalls some of her thoughts in those weeks following her husband's death:

"I felt as if I were drifting on a sea of loneliness, without a rudder, and that I had lost the captain of my ship! Or that I was stranded in the shoals of a river and the mainstream of life was passing me by.

"We so loved each other's company. He made me feel like a woman and I know I made him feel like a man—the

way we were together. I remember one day, after Bronek's death, standing at the refrigerator door. I seemed to hear my husband say to me, 'Dora, just relax and don't worry. Everything will be all right.' These were familiar words with which he often encouraged me."

That moment at the refrigerator door seemed to have been a freeing moment. It is a lonely thought that has to be faced: the end of a life together. Still, it must be faced because it is reality and we are provided somehow with the necessary strength as Dora received in that moment.

Dora continued:

"I felt no longer needed. When we feel no longer needed, we are no longer stimulated. Now I've learned: Never turn down an invitation. It's a door opening. When you're lonely you tend to withdraw. You think, 'No one wants to see me like this.'

"But that day I came to the drop-in was a grace. I was at my most desperate. Six months after a death is a desperate time, statistically, I found out later. And Saturday night is the loneliest night of the week. But I had reached the stage of wondering which was worse: to stay home alone or go out and face coming home to an empty apartment.

"Anyway, that day, I saw the 'Open House' sign so I just went in. It was the first glimmer as I thought: 'Maybe I can help someone.'

"I went in and you were there. You greeted me and said, 'Come and sit at my table,' and we had tea. Later I met Father Joe and I came to Mass there. Gradually I knew what it feels like to be alive again. I thought, 'Maybe I can reach out to others as you reached out to me.' I got involved serving coffee there. Then I went to a Sharon Family Peace Weekend and I knew you and my sister's family who were there."[3]

As she recalled that year, I was watching Dora's face, the face of a woman alive, full of purpose, handsomely dressed in shades of rose, attractive, with great kindness in her manner. I was full of admiration, too, since I knew that Dora had taken the initiative, out of the experience of her own loneliness, to join Community Contacts for the Widowed and for six years to help countless widows as they came together in the loneliness they shared. She explains:

"One hard part for me was I didn't want to be a widow or to be always with women. But I decided I must do it. I must get to be happy with and among women. Learn to be happy with women because that is who I am now. Actually get back and begin to enjoy being with other women. It doesn't rule out beginning to date or possible remarriage.

In the end, I realized I could help other women who have lost spouses, and not only women but men. You have to stimulate your creativity to interact with others whether on the social level, work level, committees, religious level, whatever."

At the time of this interview, Dora was working on a series of talks for self-help to bereaved spouses sponsored by Family Services Association of Metro Toronto. I quote her from the daily paper:

> People who are grieving should be aware that all those strange feelings they're having are normal.[...] The difference between widows and widowers is that women are more apt to find a new social life with other women, which is a great support. Widowers are not able to express their feelings about grief. They like to project the image of being strong, yet their pain is the same.[4]

Another woman who was also working with the same agency is Sylvia, mother of seven, left widowed in 1975 when her youngest child was five. I spoke with her of her own personal experience of being widowed. She told me:

"My sense of loneliness, the way it hit me, was the sense of not being first in anyone else's life. I identified that feeling only about six years ago when I realized the children were all grown and really didn't need me that much. My parents both died within the same year, five years after my husband.

"I had been an only child. So I think that is the essence of loneliness for me. The temptation is to become selfish and think, 'Since no one else cares about me, I have to care for myself'—implying not caring for anyone else! But you have to keep reaching out. It's like a full-time job just keeping contacts. They don't come to you; you have to go to them."

The image of loneliness for Sylvia seemed to be a sunny Sunday afternoon with no one with whom to do something, or enjoy a wonderful day. Sylvia quickly assured me that her family are very caring and thoughtful for her, but naturally they have their own life and other friends. She also said that, because of her family history, she knows how to adjust and is quite flexible:

"My parents were immigrants and my husband was a refugee from Czechoslovakia. My parents moved a lot and travelled. There were many goodbyes and separations in my life from the start. And one tends to build walls to protect oneself from further separation, not to get intimate so as not to suffer the separation. Because of my background, I find I have great empathy with refugees and with the feeling of not belonging."

Sylvia has turned over her basement apartment to refugee families. She feels a certain "call" to help ease them into their new culture and help them make contacts and friends. And she does it very well.

Sylvia also told of visiting her husband's mother in Czechoslovakia in 1978 and seeing on the wall the picture of all her children. She recalled going to church and realizing that many of these people knew her husband and had prayed for his safety as he escaped from his homeland.

"I realized that part of my life was here, that this was the meaning of the Mystical Body of Christ and the Communion of Saints—and I found myself crying; but it was good."

As she reflected about this family history, we both sensed how important it is for the one left behind by the death of a spouse to pick up the threads of life, to appreciate the fabric, as it were, in order to be in touch with his or her own resources and assets and to understand better the pain of separation. It is important to remember personal histories, not in order to live backwards, but to see one's life as a whole and this separation as a part of the whole.

Sylvia made another point:

"When you lose your spouse in death, you also lose a lifestyle. It's a big change. Your new lifestyle tries to replace the loss... something it doesn't, but you try to adjust.

"It happens, too, as with my husband dying of cancer, that the separation starts even before death. While Jerry was in hospital the last time, we were going two different paths and there was nothing we could do to prevent that distancing. As I recall, C.S. Lewis wrote something to that effect in A Grief Observed. 'Illness,' he said, 'separates like a policeman directing traffic: you go this way, you go that way.' And you must go."

Sylvia spoke also of the relationship with her children:

"There may be a deep loneliness because the children express their grief perhaps in rebellious behaviour or refuse to talk about it. A mother may rely too much on her older children. It is unfair to expect them to take on adult responsibility for which they are not ready or to take on the burden of your own grief, or somehow to replace your husband emotionally. The spouse has invested so much more time and emotion in the relationship with the one who has died, in ways the children do not understand. Sometimes the children don't understand why you don't 'get over it' and this makes one feel very lonely.

"On the other hand, older children may think they have to take care of you, take charge and protect you, whereas, as a parent, you want to maintain independence and charge of your own life.

"Then again, you just may not want to talk about the loneliness for fear of burdening the children."

What I call this inequality of grief on the parts of widow(er) and children is pointedly expressed in a poem by Edna St. Vincent Millay:

Lament

> Listen, children,
> Your father is dead.
> I'll make you little jackets;
> I'll make you little trousers
> From his old pants.
> There'll be in his pockets

Things he used to put there,
Keys and pennies
Covered with tobacco;
Dan shall have the pennies
To save in his bank;
Anne shall have the keys
To make a pretty noise with.
Life must go on,
And the dead be forgotten;
Life must go on,
Though good men die;
Anne, eat your breakfast,
Dan, take your medicine;
Life must go on;
I forget just why.

The bereaved spouse will want to keep some article of clothing, an old sweater, a bathrobe. And the child of fifteen may say, "What are you keeping that old thing for?" My sister, recently widowed, packed away her husband's clothing to give to the St. Vincent de Paul Society for the poor, but she said to me:

"You know, it's funny. I just couldn't pack his shoes. I wonder why I couldn't pack his shoes. None of the kids will wear them. But I just couldn't put them into that box."

And I said to her:

"Maybe because no one can ever fill his shoes?"

Eventually she was able to give them away.

Separated and divorced

Some might wonder why the loneliness of the bereaved and that of the separated and divorced are included in the same chapter. Do they belong together? The question is answered by a member of a support group for separated, divorced and widowed persons:

"What do I as a widowed person have in common with the divorced person? As a widowed person I received the flowers and the cards, and many caring, helping and understanding people reaching out to me. For divorced persons the grief is just the same, painful and lonely. But, they don't receive the cards and flowers."

Separation of any kind, I have discovered, bears a resemblance to death. My discovery came with the following experiences.

I watched my father die. I heard his breath go out. Especially I saw his strong hands die. As I watched, I had the sense of this body having fathered me physically and this person having fathered me personally. Something of each of us was in the other. So I felt something within me die with him, as if my insides were gone. The nurses offered us coffee but I could not drink because I had no place to put it.... I had no insides. For about two and a half hours I was in this physical state of emptiness. In my mind I felt like a small boat on a very large ocean, launched out there alone for the first time, having to take the rudder and not sure how to do it. It was unbearably lonely. For one thing, I did not feel that my brothers and sisters were experiencing just what I was experiencing and I despaired both of explaining it and of recovering from it. I was alone in the boat, with no one near to help. Only when I began to prepare for bed did I become aware of a new presence of my father, assuring me: "I am still your dad. I am still with you." Then tears began to flow and, with them, consolation.

When I returned from my father's funeral, I was greeted by many in sympathy. It was lonely because, oddly perhaps, my loneliness was increased by the greetings. I wanted to say,

"But it doesn't really matter to you. You can't understand because he wasn't your father. You are not in my place. It hasn't changed your life. You didn't even know him."

I was able to share this feeling with a close friend of mine in the community, one who had had a very difficult relationship with her parents and therefore a difficult experience of her father's death. She said to me:

"Thank God for this pain. I wish I could have loved my father so as to have experienced at his death the pain you are having. I envy you."

At this period in my life I had developed a close friendship with someone I had worked with. Visits were few because of geography, but on one occasion in particular when he came for a conference, we had time for a good sharing of life, prayer and hopes. After his departure, I felt for days an emptiness and loss that was physically draining. I slowly became aware that it was indeed the same physical, psychological and spiritual phenomenon that I had had at my father's death. I was mourning. It was then that I realized that mourning, separation and loneliness are all related.

In separation and divorce, the division is as real and usually as permanent as that caused by death. The failure of an intimate relationship is a great grief, accompanied by great loneliness. Fortunately, this is now recognized and help is being given to move through the process of New Beginnings, the name of a program for widowed, separated and divorced Christians.[5] Often the loneliness begins long before the separation takes place. As one wife put it, "When he comes home, my loneliness begins." The terrible awareness of the rift pervades.

After the separation, there is the adjustment to living alone or as a one-parent family, even while there may also be a certain relief as in the case of violence in the relationship. Often there are doubts about whether the right decision was made, or if something more could have been done. Usually the decision has been a personal and isolated one, though more today are taking advantage of counselling.

I interviewed some persons who have undergone this kind of separation. I asked them, "What is your image of loneliness?"

Judith's answer was:

"I picture a St. John's saltwater beach in autumn. It is abandoned. In summer it was colourful, beach balls were bouncing, there were lots of people. It was a sort of community fun place.

"Now it is desolate. Everyone is gone."

Frances replied to the question:

"I picture a person in a catatonic state, arms folded, back-to-back withdrawal. It's scary. The person has sort of stopped living and relapsed into him or herself."

Keith's image was the picture of a family together at the Exhibition or at Christmas:

"I feel I'd rather work holidays, especially Christmas. I'm glad when the stores stop playing the Christmas carols."

All of these images have the common element of feeling isolated. As Kay said:

"I ask myself: 'Why am I lonely when I can pick up the phone and talk to one of the girls or one of my friends?' But there's something inside that's impossible to share."

In telling her story of separation and divorce, Judith spoke of the desolation of spirit. She felt disconnected with the rest of humanity and, for a time, with God. Yet she remembered also how, before the separation, though she endured for five or six years after the children had all left home, she was haunted by the thought, "I will never be happy again in my life, ever." There was no light at the end of the tunnel. Her account continued:

"I got my driver's license which gave me some mobility, as I was a long distance from church. I started therapy and wanted my husband to come with me. He came twice but refused to continue, saying I was to blame and it was my problem. I made up my mind to be happy whether it meant go or stay.

"People around were not reading my signals. As far as I was concerned, the whole world was 'out.'

"I did a lot of searching. Through a priest and a therapist I learned a lot about myself, a lot that I could love and like. That was important because my self-image was really battered.

"One thing I came to realize: my happiness had to depend on me, not on him—my husband. I was hostile and angry and so was he. But it became a question of survival.

"I was teaching through all this. In my worst year, the principal of the school was wonderful. He said, 'If you need a break, a mental health day, take it.' I didn't need to, but just knowing the offer was there helped.

"Finally, I made the decision to go on my own. My husband was both glad and mad: glad to get rid of me, I think, but mad because he had a high profile and it was embarrassing.

"I had anxieties after I left but when I made contact with my husband over the phone, I knew it was right. At one point I felt a panic but I talked for three hours with a friend. It was a turning point. I stood on my own. I was soon able to stop therapy."

Judith is the picture of a happy, determined, capable professional person who obviously has a new lease on life. She was doing some funded research on a sabbatical from teaching when I met her. As we shared about our work, I told her about this book, and she offered her story. We discussed more deeply her experience of and coping with loneliness following her separation. Judith explained:

"There are two levels of loneliness: the personal and the social. My isolation from God is gone now. And I do not think of God as male but as God.

"On the social level, I felt ostracized. My mother did not want anyone to know about my divorce and she wondered what she had done wrong in raising us. That was very lonely for her and for me.

"It was really my women friends who helped me. They did not let me withdraw but dragged me kicking and screaming into the real world. Now we can be friends and share on the spiritual level. Celibacy evolved naturally. But people say things, assume things, leer.

"I've also experienced an even more profound loneliness that results from taking an unpopular stand on behalf of someone else. It's the kind of loneliness that people working in justice and peace experience. But you get the strength from the very source of your life.

"There's a joy in overcoming the fear. I feel connectedness now."

Judith's phrase, "into the real world," is a telling one. It is the very reality of living that is healing for those whose world has been shattered by separation and divorce. Kay, whose separation was sudden and shocking, said:

"I felt so guilty. How come I didn't notice? Maybe if I had... maybe... maybe.... Failure is when you didn't try. God knows I tried.

"But I'm down to reality now. This is the way it is now. Reality and God have been the saving grace."

The way Keith put it was, "I feel I have more solidity now."

Frances spoke of the "temptation" to leave the real world and lapse into the catatonic state. Eugene Kennedy, who also wrote on loneliness, speaks of a sort of reality therapy:

"There is simply no healing agent for being human that is any better than the steady, active and realistic insertion of ourselves into life."[6]

Frances managed to stay in the real world. She shared at length with me her own experience, moving back and forth between theological musings and descriptions of the concrete experience. Speaking of loneliness itself, Frances remarked:

"Loneliness is self-pity. That's the disease of loneliness. It is partly because we attribute loneliness to rejection. It is thought of as a punishment: you're made to stand in the corner, segregated from others, or told to leave the room, or made to go to your room. To be alone becomes a bad thing; solitary confinement is a punishment. So you never learn to be alone, in a good sense.

"I was a lonely only child and very shy. In retrospect, I think I was a tactile child who needed cuddling, and my upbringing was a far cry from that. It's like having something lacking in your diet! I never knew my father, only my stepfather, and I always was a sort of Cinderella.

"But so was my mother. She was brought from England by an aunt; but then there was a baby and my mother became the maid. I know she felt rejected. Through my own journey I have come to feel a deep compassion and love for her. The rejection she felt led her to demand perfection from me.

"I married young, a man twelve years older than me. I wanted to get away and have my own family. When my husband left, it was a relief and I kept the children."

These last remarks came as a surprise to me since I knew that the separation was not the end of her troubles. And Frances responded to my questions about parenting alone:

"I think for me the worst of going it alone was the lack of family support. I did have my grandmother who, though not a warm and affectionate person, was there. She represented for me order and stability. Crisis lines are excellent. If you know someone is coming, you can hang on."

Frances explained how she had worked as a real estate secretary and been able, with help, to begin buying a house and setting up a small business, a boutique. Things looked promising:

"Also in the late sixties, early seventies, I met and became friends with a man. When his wife died, he spoke of marriage with me, sure that it was meant to be. Just when I accepted, he died suddenly. I also lost my house and business.

"I was angry. I felt it was 'fate.' I felt abandoned. What did I do to get this? Why? Nothing in my previous experience prepared me for these events. Worst of all, I really had no faith to draw on. I saw God as a mean-spirited God who only interfered with my happiness—right from birth.

"And yet, every time I looked at my two beautiful sons, I saw him."

Frances was expressing what many people have experienced: this feeling of being betrayed even by God, certainly by life! It is an immense task to deal with this perceived abandonment. In the end, if one is open, one also perceives that the very One who seems to have betrayed us is the One who comes to our rescue. Frances had the added pain of a distancing from her son at the time of a grandchild's birth. Yet even then, consolation came in the form of a beautiful four-year-old child she was asked to care for during some months. Paul was an affectionate and precocious child, indeed a gift of God. Another godsend for Frances were three friends, Ollie, Gail, and Gail's mother.

Frances began to speak positively about what helped her out of loneliness:

"The best help is one who knows. My friend Ollie understood my pain. But then I started to get very busy. The tendency for a lonely person may be to get very busy in all sorts of activities, volunteering, etc. Even my two best friends didn't realize I was running from instead of facing my loneliness. The opposite extreme is to remain alienated and immobilized. But one has to get connected again. I decided: 'I'm a social being, not a bleeding heart!'

"I used my experience as a resource. One can be more objective and understanding because of what one has been through. At present I am working at a family daycare centre. I feel I can help.

"I read a lot. I love cultural experiences. I have a lot of spiritual helps. St. Vincent de Paul Society is very important to me. We talk with each other and share as well as help others.

"I'm determined to keep reaching out. Otherwise I won't find life."

Some weeks after our conversation, I met Frances again. She told me:

"Recently I've been getting some spiritual counselling from a Jesuit. He has sort of walked me through my past with Jesus present in and at each of the moments of hurt. I feel a real relationship with Jesus as my brother and my friend. I never had that before."

Frances was able to let go of resentment and anger that she had long harboured and which had affected her physical health. She laughed and concluded:

"You know what! I discovered that by forgiving them—God included—I freed myself."

I feel sure that Frances will be less lonely and more happily connected from here on.

Keith's story shows the experience of loneliness from a man's viewpoint. Keith used to come to our house to celebrate liturgy when he was going through a divorce. At the time, we did not speak about it much but we sensed his suffering and welcomed him among us, hoping that he would take strength and consolation from our gathering together in eucharist.

Keith agreed to share his story. At first, he spoke more of the stress than of the loneliness of his separation and divorce. In fact, I thought he was not really in touch with his loneliness until I questioned him a little. The separation had taken him somewhat by surprise:

"It was very stressful. I couldn't believe it was happening. I hadn't seen what was going on. I was so busy with work, sports, a lot of things—money, a home... I thought I was providing well [and he was].

"I guess you have to go through the eye of the needle to mature. I think I was pretty immature about marriage. I learned a lot about myself through the breakup. I guess I always saw everything in plain black and white.

"When I was going through all this, I kept in shape—that helped. I ran. But then I ran too much, did marathons. I got depleted, I guess. I was also running away. I'd get very high running, then very low.

"I wouldn't say I was feeling lonely; I was more frustrated. I couldn't get what I wanted—I always had, I guess. But I did everything wrong in this case.

"My family stood by me. Your friends—you find out who your friends are. They fall like cordwood. I felt 100% wrong on the breakup. I felt here I was mid-fifties—frustrated that I hadn't always done as well as I should have, even in getting promoted at work. I didn't give it my best."

I asked Keith what helped him.

"I read a lot. *The Consolation of Philosophy* by Boethius. You wouldn't understand it until you went through suffering. Religion helped—hurt first, then helped. I had left it behind. I was 'left of dogmatic' but it turned out to be important. It helped me not to be so up and down, high and low.

"I feel I've got more solidity now.

"Cursillo helped—helps analyze. Lots of lonely people there. They want me to give more leadership but I feel burnt out."

The conversation began to drift away from what helped to what did not:

"At work, I don't socialize that much. Firemen seem to me to talk money a lot. I suppose I did, too, before. Different values now. But I'm also a bit of a loner in a crowd anyway. I'm moody. I guess sometimes I told my story over and over to too many at work. A sort of 'poor me' tale. I suppose I was looking for support when I was going through the divorce. It turned people off. I felt loneliness there I guess. They advised me to leave my wife alone, cool it out. I didn't take their advice and that was a mistake.

"But some said, 'Get a girlfriend.' My own moral precepts didn't allow that. There's no happiness just in sex—using each other. Usually they want you to come and live with them.

"Also, I'm very honest, very blunt, and that can turn people off. I'm trying to temper it.

"I started neglecting things. I was uptight, on pins and needles. I'd stay in my room on my days off... neglect myself. Then I'd say to myself: 'This isn't good. Get movin'!'

"I guess this was my first big defeat."

That was the key word as to how Keith was describing his feelings and his experience. He didn't use the word "lonely" at first, but defeat is a lonely thing. We are back to rejection and nobody likes a 'loser.'

I recalled Keith back to what had helped:

"I made a retreat at Marylake. It's hard, very hard to get good spiritual direction.[...] I guess I do experience loneliness—I'm not a yuppie, I'm not a family man now, and there's sort of no place for me in society.[...] You have a community: that's important. I went to my nephew's for a while, but he's a family man and I didn't feel I belonged. I'd go and then come back feeling negative."

I asked about his relationship with his children:

"I've told them this breakup isn't their fault, not to blame themselves. But they remind me... I don't know if we should keep contact...They say fathers often don't maintain contact."

I encouraged Keith to keep in touch but I felt there was still a great deal of pain to be worked through. He is taking the right steps and making great efforts. There is an honesty in him, trying to see the way and to do what is best. Keith is not yet able to close this chapter of his life and so he would be an excellent candidate for New Beginnings.

A word about New Beginnings, both as an organization and as a philosophy. I have noted above that several persons remarked that reality has been both a means and a result of their coping with loneliness following a separation. Reality is at the heart of New Beginnings, a weekend program started by Sister Jean de Luca originally for widows, but now embracing all adult victims of separation. The slogan of New Beginnings is: "Look back, Reach out, Move on." In other words, face the loneliness and hurt, share with others, and begin a new life.

As Sister Jean says:

"We need to help people look at their own situation. There has been a drastic change in their lives. They need to know how to pick up the pieces and get on with living—to cope with being alone."

She emphasizes that the weekend program is not a garbage dumping session but a dealing with unfinished business, learning to forgive, let go and get on with new choices. It is a "closure on the past and a new beginning in the present." As Eleanor McCombes says,

"It doesn't answer all life's problems but has a guiding influence in looking at the future, while gently closing the door on the past."

Eleanor made the program after being prematurely widowed, and she now works with Sister Jean. Other comments from participants indicate that the group support is important:

- "I feel great support from my group—the feeling of isolation faded out of my life."
- "My depression has lifted. I now feel I can mix with others, take my place in society."
- "The best thing about the program is the sharing. Many men feel awkward about sharing or even showing their emotions, but I found myself not afraid to open discussion. It's just opened a whole new door."

People learn that their loneliness is normal but also that something can be done about it. People learn to let go of self-defeating attitudes and to choose life-giving ones.

Scriptural consolation

We have seen that facing loneliness, sharing with others who have had a similar experience and reaching out to help others are all part of weathering separation loneliness and of reconnecting. The reconnecting and even reconciliation with God are paramount steps especially for Christians, because the sense of being abandoned may be strong.

We must know that God is walking with us in our own places of desolation. Humans fail, but God does not. As God tells us through Jeremiah: "I have loved you with an everlasting love" (Jeremiah 31:3).

Indeed we are all unable to be faithful without fail. The entire book of Hosea portrays us, God's own beloved people, as failures in fidelity contrasted with God's faithfulness. Chapter 16 of Ezekiel again compares us all to a deliberately unfaithful wife because we break the covenant with God. But at the same time it assures us that God will make a new covenant with us. The story of God's promise to the House of David (2 Samuel 7) is that God's love will never fail. It will correct the sins of the household, but it will never be withdrawn. Isaiah consoles us with the words:

> No more shall people call you "Forsaken,"
> or your land "Desolate,"
> but you shall be called "My delight,"
> and your land "Espoused."
> For the Lord delights in you,
> and makes your land his spouse.
> As a young man marries a virgin,
> your Builder will marry you.
>
> (Isaiah 62:4-5)

The scripture is written for our instruction and consolation. If God so loves sinful people, how compassionate must God be toward those who have undergone the desolation and pain of separation.

Further, we see Jesus' great compassion for the widow who has now lost her only son (Luke 7). So moved was he that he raised the boy from death and gave him back to his mother. If he does not do so in our case, it is not because he loves us less. Perhaps we forget, too, that the bleeding woman who touched the hem of his garment was an outcast, unclean, forbidden to enter the Temple, considered unfit to worship. Yet by that hidden touch, power went out from him to heal her (Luke 8). If Jesus has hard words about divorce and about the hardness of our hearts, he never says he does not forgive our failures, for he came that we might have life abundantly (John 10:10). Jesus was not talking about people who have no troubles!

There comes to mind that little story about the two sets of foot-prints in the sand in the journey along the shore of life, a journey with God. Looking back after a difficult stretch, the walker sees a space of the journey where there is only one set of footprints and complains to God, "Where were you when I was in trouble? When I was so alone in my walking?" And the reply comes, "I was carrying you."

Lessening loneliness

- Stay with reality. Neither idealize the lost one nor denigrate the left one, nor deny your pain.
- Face the loneliness and acknowledge it as human.
- Share with others who have gone through or are going through similar separation loneliness. Find or form a community of persons with whom to share.
- Reach out to others even when you feel like withdrawing.
- Accept invitations extended to you (unless it is imprudent to do so).
- Try not to neglect yourself, your appearance, your health.
- Do not carry guilt around. It grows heavy by being carried. Take steps to resolve it.
- In the words of New Beginnings: "Look back, Reach out, Move on."
- Know that your experience can become a help to others. Time does heal, but you may need assistance in order for that healing to occur.
- Write for "Parenting Alone," "Loneliness," and other related topics: *Christopher News Notes*, 12 East 48th St., New York, NY 10017. (Free: donations appreciated.)
- Contact New Beginnings and/or the Canadian Association for Separated and Divorced Catholics, or inquire into such groups in your locality.
- Pray. God does not condemn or abandon you but always gives life.

The loneliness of "Religion"

This chapter might have been entitled "Celibate Loneliness" except that, in reality, loneliness is not the preserve of celibates but is common in pastoral ministry to both the married and the unmarried. "The vocation has loneliness built into it," writes Arnold Weigel of Waterloo Lutheran Seminary in an article entitled "Loneliness among Ministers."[1] This chapter will consider all forms of religious life as these are affected by loneliness.

The above-mentioned article opens with a description of a hectic day of telephone calls, hospital emergencies, wedding rehearsal, church council meeting and dinner with the community social worker. It ends with the return home, only to find that the family have all gone to bed... not an unusual situation for the minister.

Loneliness seems to have something to do with a lack in our relationships with others, with God or with ourselves. Religious ministry is filled with relationships but most of these are helping relationships, which may be rather one-way. Little time may remain for the receiving relationships of family or friends and these may indeed wither if they ever get to exist at all. The resources of the minister are not endless. Who ministers to the minister? Or as the saying goes, "Who is guru to the guru?"

There are relational hazards in the life and work of those in religion. These include the tyranny of expectations, the difficulty of preaching from conviction, the loneliness of responsibility, burnout, and the indifference of the faithful.

First, the tyranny of expectations, trying to be all things to all people and feeling guilty or inadequate when it becomes impossible by sheer force of numbers or workload or plain disagreement. The expectations may be on either the part of others or the minister's.

Second, preaching itself may put a distance between the minister and the flock. The preacher may feel inhibited from expressing real conviction, or may not receive genuine feedback and be left in doubt as to the depth of his effectiveness.

Third, there is a problem of loneliness at the top, even when there is good team ministry, because the pastor has the ultimate responsibility, at least according to the present structures and in the minds of people. This is not to mention confidentiality or the privacy of "confession" which has been carried to the extreme in the Catholic tradition which in the early centuries knew nothing but public penance.

Fourth, the numerous meetings the minister must attend can become like a treadmill and lose their meaningfulness. One can be lonely in a crowd. One can end up feeling like a functionary rather than a person. Indeed, who of us when overextended does not feel like "pitching the whole thing"? A recent study,[2] indicates that the main reason priests resign is neither burnout nor celibacy but dissatisfaction and meaninglessness in their work. Fully two-thirds of those polled said that the lack of challenge and use of their human potential (i.e. repetitiveness and boredom) was primary in their decision to leave the ministry. Only 29% said they would have remained in ministry if allowed to marry. The sequence was: dissatisfaction, loneliness, desire to marry; not the reverse. When work becomes dull necessity with little creativity, the result is fatal.

Fifth, built into religious endeavour is the desire and hope for the ideal and prophetic element. If the minister is living the prophetic role, he or she often feels isolated, unpopular and even rejected. Finally, or at least from time to time, such a person may well succumb to the Jeremiah or Elijah syndrome, which in popular jargon would be, "God, I've had it!" In scriptural language, the feeling would be:

> Is there not balm in Gilead?
> Is there no doctor here?
> Then why does it make no progress,
> This cure of the daughter of my people?
> ...
> Who will find me a wayfarer's shelter in the desert,
> for me to quit my people,
> and leave them far behind?
> For all of them are adulterers,
> a conspiracy of traitors.
> ...
> They have accustomed their tongues to lying
> they are corrupt, incapable of repentance.
>
> Fraud after fraud, deceit after deceit! (Jeremiah 8)

Or again, admitting that Jeremiah was inclined to exaggerate a little in his weariness:

> I am a daily laughingstock,
> everybody's butt.
> ...
> The word of God has meant for me
> insult, derision, all day long. (Jeremiah 20)

Elijah before him had experienced this weariness too. At the threats of Jezebel:

He himself went into the wilderness, a day's journey, and sitting under a furze bush wished he were dead.

"Yahweh," he said, "I have had enough. Take my life; I am no better than my ancestors." Then he lay down and went to sleep.

(1 Kings 19)

Perhaps those most zealous about social change and justice and the visibility of the Reign of God experience this loneliness of the "indifference of the faithful" most deeply or, worse, their infidelity to the gospel ideals. To try to broaden the vision and elucidate the meaning of the gospel in our time can be very discouraging and may cause the minister to feel alone indeed, to the point of not seeing the good that is there.

Father Tom

We are not considering here only the reasons why ministers resign, but also the stories of those who continue on their way even while acknowledging the fact of loneliness in their lives. I spoke with some of these who shared generously with me. One of these persons was Father Tom McKillop, founder of Youth Corps and now pastor of a parish in Toronto.

We had a breakfast meeting: this is a busy man! We chatted and got caught up on recent happenings but soon we were into the topic. I plunged in with the question: "What image comes to mind for you when I say 'loneliness'?" and I was surprised by the answer:

"My symbol of loneliness is stuttering. From early on, I had this trouble, an inability to feel at ease, to communicate. I felt blocked off. I'd never know if I tried to speak whether it would come out or not. From the age of fifteen to thirty-one, especially with heterosexual relationships, I felt this. So I got into sports and excelled there. It was action and tasks, not relationships.

"I got into the habit of asking questions and receiving answers, not the other way around. I avoided being asked

since I might not be able to answer because of the stuttering. I had to ask, but I felt blocked because I couldn't participate in the conversation.

"I wrote bits of poetry, somewhat embarrassingly, to express what I was feeling. It seemed like a sort of contradiction—a ball player writing poetry. My mother was affirming but I still feared it was inappropriate. But writing was a way to communicate what was within me.

"What I would tend to do is maybe go to a dance hall or wherever, look in and then walk away. I'd withdraw, afraid I couldn't speak. At least in sports there were adults who believed in me, affirmed and freed me, but always underneath was the deep desire for friendship."

Although I knew Fr. Tom had this affliction, so well has he overcome it that I could really only recall once when I saw him faltering. We talked about that night at Central Tech when he was giving out diplomas to the handicapped who had successfully completed their courses. I told him how I had sat there praying he would get through; he said it was a horror. Only the presence of Leonard Cheshire on stage with him gave him the courage to go on. (Leonard Cheshire was one of the overseers in the bomber that levelled Hiroshima and Nagasaki with nuclear bombs. He later became the founder of the Cheshire Homes for the handicapped.)

"I had to learn to relax before speaking, especially the mouth and throat. And you need a strong motivation, like 'I really want to say this. I want to be out there.' The breakthrough came at Varsity Stadium with Mother Teresa. There were 20,000 people. I sat there, bowed my head and tried to reflect within myself. I was saying slowly, 'Jesus, Jesus.' Then the words came: 'Don't be afraid.' I said to myself: 'O.K. This is it! Do it!'

"After I had done it—got up and spoke—I knew finally it was conquered. I'd never look back."

I proceeded then to ask Fr. Tom a rather intimate question which I thought was important in terms of vocation and loneliness. I asked him if he had ever thought that his choice of vocation had been based, at least in part, on fear of not being able to succeed in relating with women because of his speech problem. He told me briefly of his relationships with three women when he was in his twenties and a single teacher. There were certainly possibilities but these relationships, he said, lacked the depth he sought. True, coming through all boys' schools had not made it any easier to relate to girls. Again, before entering St. Augustine's Seminary, he met a beautiful person while volunteering. The relationship could well have developed into a deep friendship, even another choice. But Fr. Tom did make a real choice to enter St. Augustine's:

"It was a choice in keeping with a religious experience I had had at twenty-six. That experience had stayed with me. At thirty-one I had entered the Paulists. I felt Jesus was very real. But I was too intense and the speech problem was bad. I became a 'case.' Finally, I was told to leave. It might have been shattering but a priest gave me some good advice. He told me to do four things: see a priest for direction when I got back; get a job; socialize; and volunteer for some project. What it meant was: Don't think of yourself as a seminarian and don't give in to self-pity.

"So when I entered St. Augustine's Seminary, it wasn't primarily to become a priest. It was really to follow that foundational experience I had had at twenty-six. I was led to prayer, to the relationship with Jesus.

"I was older. I drew the younger ones out, went from one to another in personal conversation and affirmed each one. I wanted to help each one to be a priest, whether I myself was ever to be ordained or not. I wondered if I was there simply for the others. It meant being a person rather than playing a role. I resolved to be myself, to be Tom McKillop. That's all I could ever be. The role was gone, the role of trying to be what fitted. 'If they ever ordain me,' I thought, 'they'll know what they are getting.'

"I raised questions and sought to become aware through social action. My academic career flourished. I began to risk. I just thought, 'If Jesus wants me, he wants me as I am.' It became not my will but a response to an invitation."

This account might sound as if the problems were gone, the stuttering overcome, the loneliness fled. I knew it was not so for the breakthrough at Varsity Stadium had come much later. So I pressed my question:

"As a priest, then, have you experienced loneliness, and in what way?"

Fr. Tom continued:

"I always had that fear and tension before I had to speak or preach. Fear is the clue to loneliness. Also if you don't feel at peace, if you're not 'together,' it is a great obstacle. You tend to withdraw then. You have to be physically, emotionally and spiritually integrated. You have to wrestle with all three. You can't deal with just one. I've said before there are three enemies we have: loneliness, fear and guilt. We're not free under these. Loneliness is cured by friendship, fear by trusting others and your own capacities, guilt by forgiveness and action."

Fr. Tom has put his theories so well into practice that I wanted him to tell more of his experience and to give words of advice for others struggling with loneliness or the kinds of afflictions that lead to great loneliness. I knew his real concern for fellow priests and for youth. He has done so many concrete actions to show this concern. I recalled, for example, how he put his mother's house, which he inherited at her death, at the service of priests so that they would have a common place to gather on days off in order to pray, relax and share; few took advantage of it. But Fr. Tom is now a member of a monthly reflection-sharing time with priests who come together for mutual upbuilding.

His work with youth is legendary both as founder of Youth Corps and one-to-one as a personal friend and adviser to youth.[3] I asked him, as we neared the end of our breakfast meeting: "What advice would you pass on about dealing with loneliness?" I have condensed his answer:

"You turn your handicap into an asset. In my case, I knew that I knew how to listen to youth. I empathize with them: they are figuratively 'stuttering alone.' They have difficulty with being alone and the three enemies of which I spoke can lead them to suicide. The cry for relationship is desperate and powerful in youth. When I am around youth, I sense their loneliness. I can smell loneliness, detect it in the young. You have to be with them and allow them to trust you and then share. I learned to go to them through activities.

"About priests and hyperstress: a lot of things were summed up for me at a workshop for priests given by Dr. Fraser from the Clark Institute. For example: eat properly,

three meals a day—take time. Jog. Take limited amounts of alcohol. Get the proper amount of sleep—that helps. Make sure you have time and space for meditation, to keep in touch within. Then he highlighted, held up on a separate card, the word 'Friendship.' He said you really need a friend you can share with—share hopes, dreams, fears, secrets. You have to risk communication. Communication is essential. Otherwise you get guilt, burnout, deprivation of touch, especially when we get into our past-55 stage, when our parents are gone and we don't have family or human community. We are judged by our productivity. We become the 'hermit functionary.'"

Without interrupting I thought of how great was the bond between Fr. Tom and his mother. She lived to a good age but her death left him with no immediate family. When we spoke of his mother, Fr. Tom told how, in the last two weeks of her dying, John Howard Griffin returned to Toronto. It was some years since they had met. John accompanied Tom through some of those last days. He took a remarkable photograph of Mrs. McKillop and was just there with Tom. There sprang up what Fr. Tom called "an incredible friendship," one that endured and deepened to the end of John Howard's life in 1980. Fr. Tom was able to share deeply with this man. The overlap of time when Fr. Tom was saying goodbye to his mother and hello again to John Howard was what I call an epiphany—a revelation of God's action and presence, just as a true friend is always the gift of God. Fr. Tom later went to Texas to share a sort of retreat with John and the exchange of letters kept them in touch. As Fr. Tom said, "I think you could say John became for me the brother I never had. It was the friendship I had always so deeply desired from way back."

And it was a friendship able to be shared with so many of us who know both of these remarkable men.

Fr. Tom concluded our meeting with some less personal words:

"We were warned about having particular friendships but it's Catch-22. If you have no support group to share deeply with, you're just as badly off. Most of us live in cocoons: we emerge a bit and go back in. We fear the change, so we stay a caterpillar or, at best, a moth, instead of becoming the butterfly that flies free.

"We need to develop some teaching on spiritual friendship. There are lots of examples among the saints and in the gospel. We need to learn how to be friends."

Though our long breakfast was coming to an end, I felt we were just getting started! As we parted, I asked Fr. Tom, "May I use your name, or do you want to be anonymous?"

True to his principles and practice, he answered:

"Tell it like it is! You can use my name!"

I believe that willingness to "tell it like it is" is part of the success of overcoming loneliness.

Fr. Tom McKillop is a priest in the largest city in Canada. Living in the great pulsing heart of such a metropolis with its perpetual motion is no guarantee, as we have seen, against loneliness. Neither is the multiple-mission situation of some of the more remote areas of a large country. Many priests have lived alone for years, far from family or large population centres. There has been loneliness, more for some than others. Some become part of their people more than others. In any case, the celibate lifestyle of the priest or the religious mission itself sets the minister apart from the common humanity shared by everyone. A certain remoteness caused by people's attitudes adds to the barrenness of the internal landscape.

Father Emil: In the belly of the whale

In the interior of British Columbia, a priest is assigned several towns stretching from Kamloops to Valemount, with a provincial prison added in. Fr. Emil has spent a number of years of his life there. I knew he knew what loneliness was, even though he is a "people person" and has little spare time in the midst of his travels of ministry. His story seemed to belong in this chapter, so I approached him for it.

I have known Fr. Emil since 1972 when I was one of those community volunteers he mentions in his account. Since I could not personally interview him because of distance, I asked Fr. Emil to write something down and send it. Knowing the man and something of the experiences he has lived through, knowing that the mission setting was a perfect circumstance for loneliness, I hoped to share his reflections in this chapter. I sent some questions to stimulate Fr. Emil's reflection, questions which no doubt were quite unnecessary. The image of the mountain wilderness is a powerful one. The mountain was the beginning of the way out of the wilderness of loneliness for Fr. Emil.

April, 1988

For me, loneliness and despair are very closely linked. It was on a mountain, fighting for my life for 23 days, that I faced my loneliness for the first time—I was unable to avoid it. The situation forced me to look at it since I was unable to resort to compensating or covering up as I had unwittingly learned to do.

It was my twelfth year of priesthood as a diocesan priest in the Kamloops diocese when I was forced down because of bad weather while returning to my mission in Valemount, B.C., in my two-seater homebuilt aircraft. It was high above the treeline on a steep meadow in the Cariboo mountains, alone, my plane badly damaged, unable to communicate with anyone, that I met myself and my God in ways beyond words. In that extreme survival situation I began a ten-year inner journey that demanded every bit as much of my physical and spiritual resources as did my wilderness survival.

Stripped of everything, I got my first clear insight into how my work for the Lord and his people was driven by a fear of looking at my loneliness. It was the beginning of recognizing how I subtly did everything to convince myself of my worth. Achievement, and a driving need to have it all right and acceptable, made me a slave to my pride and what I perceived as the expectations of others. I was blinded by the fact that it operated most powerfully where I was most gifted: in my deep compassion, my unshakable faith in God's desire to heal and free his people. In my caring for people, I was susceptible to using them. Unconsciously I had been seeking to fill my own needs—my need to cover over my loneliness and despair especially.

These last remarks of open admission by Fr. Emil support my conviction, from my own experience and from observation, that much if not most "apostolic work" gets done out of the needs of the person ministering: need for recognition, status, popularity, affirmation; need to keep busy with noble deeds to cover our loneliness; need of a sense of achievement and a feeling of being helpful or needed. But God makes good on these impure motives and uses the weakest instruments for his glory. It is hard for us to discern this because it is a shattering experience to realize we are unprofitable servants after all we've done!

A new awareness in Fr. Emil resulted in the discovery that he was not the only one doing good and serving people out of personal need. The "wilderness of human need" exists not only among the marginalized, but also among the lay volunteers, and in his own life.

Amazingly, from 1967 until 1975 especially, my openness to working with lay volunteers for the mission area I served sparked a tremendous response. Out of this grew a call to form parish communities at the service of the wider community through the spiritual and corporal works of mercy. Each one was invited to put his or her unique gifts at the service of God's people beginning especially with the marginalized. In the midst of that we entered a wilderness of human need requiring all the wisdom and survival techniques I had learned on the mountain—and more. It demanded a purity of heart I had not yet achieved. Only then would I be able to teach others to be totally at the service of the poor, as Jesus was.

Overwhelmed by that human wilderness and turning my life over to God in utter helplessness, a cry buried in my past began to emerge—a cry of loneliness and despair that went all the way back to my childhood.

My world fell apart when I was four years old; my childhood experience had reached a crisis point. My dad, at 45, suffered a series of strokes. The hospitalization and long convalescence was not as devastating for me as dad's attempt to take his place as head of the house again. Physically quite strong yet mentally impaired, his strong will struggled with the frustration of his handicap and the decisions my mother and older brothers had to make for the survival of the family. For 25 years the pent-up anger and frustration would strike without warning, shattering the peace of our home. As a little one, my uncertainty and dread of what might happen was greater than the actual verbal and emotional storms that would strike.

Compared to the many shattering situations we see in our world today, mine was quite manageable. But it is awesome for me to experience now that deep compassion which identified so totally with my father and mother and each member of the family. Not wanting to add to the burden of a demanding and, at times, sheer survival situation, I decided to work out all my problems or needs on my own. While this put me in touch with my God in a way I marvel at today, a whole part of me was deprived of the care and understanding my mother and family were so capable of giving me. I developed a pattern of choosing solitude more and more. I was eventually oblivious to my own needs and the immense loneliness engendered by my inability to share the deepest part of me.

After several years of carrying my family, a despair took hold of me that was so intense it affected my health. I've since relived this childhood experience of expecting to die. And worse, I had an abiding sense of worthlessness because I could not bring my family what it so desperately needed: reconciliation and peace.

A terrible frustration set in—the frustration of wanting so deeply to be able to heal, reconcile, bring peace as a person and as a priest (isn't that the "role" of the priest?), but experiencing instead an awareness of failure and of being thwarted in the attempts.

I had at the heart of me a gift of understanding and reconciliation. My sensitivity, my compassion and automatic communion with the needs of others, my reckless disregard for my own needs in the face of theirs, all continued to touch people. But always it was under the pale of my unconscious self-doubt and despair in achieving the purpose of my existence: to bring reconciliation, especially in my family. This struck at the heart of who I was as a priest. That nurtured a hidden anger buried in me that pushed me to be facetious, cynical and even harsh and precipitous. That was so contrary to my real self. It sealed my sense of isolation and loneliness.

Fr. Emil took a sabbatical and that was a time of rest and growth and direction with the help of others. He writes:

Looking back, I know if I had not maintained my communion with God, my loss would have become permanent. I'm so deeply aware of being rescued. I can taste what salvation means. I know if God hadn't sent me someone who understood me and was ready to give everything without taking anything from me, there would be no escape. If there had been no one or no place that taught me to welcome and understand my feelings, I'd still be lost. It's part of the journey of becoming a child and accepting things that I could not accept as they overwhelmed me. It is embracing the cross (i.e. weakness) as a way to life and communion. It is something I've always tried to teach but without that one element which would make my life an authentic witness. It is more and more a question of being faithful to the contemplative part in me which I lived so intensely in the impossible conditions of the mountain.

As I finished reading Fr. Emily's notes, I started to hum: "Amazing grace,... I once was lost but now I'm found, was blind but now I see." He had learned the secret of the little ones, that we are loved in our unworthiness, that God's love is unearned. Knowing that in our gut, we can give unconditional love to others, simply because it has been given to us. The greatest "apostolate" becomes our shared vulnerability and our shared grace. It is the vulnerability of the child who knows he cannot go alone, reveals his littleness and receives everything he needs. No one becomes whole alone, not even the priest. That way lies only loneliness. Fr. Emil sent along a card he carried with him always as the reminder of the way of the mountain.

"Come, give all you possess—all you are to the poor! Walk with me where life struggles to be free. My Spirit will guide you in my ways—a path in the wilderness. Do not be afraid, I am with you. Lay aside your wisdom—your strength—your old defences! Become childlike, dependent, poor, attentive and understanding with each cry.

"Take up your cross..."

This is "the call I carry," writes Fr. Emil, and it is the call he gives to all he serves in his scattered parishes along the Yellowhead in the mountainous interior of British Columbia, the call that is taking flesh in the communities where he ministers. It is a call to come out, to come together in our weakness and allow the power of Christ's love and his cross to touch and heal and unite us in him. There is no need to hide.

The call to Religion

The call to "religion" as priest, minister, brother or sister in a religious community, cloistered or "apostolic," is a call to universal love and a dedication to it. It is a call, and a gift at the same time, to a particular way of loving. In the case of a religious, this loving is done in a community whose members are all vowed to the same purpose and person, drawn by the same love who is Christ. It is a shared life, yet also a life of solitude. Solitude is not to be equated with loneliness. Still, on the way to solitude we may experience real loneliness, especially at times when spiritual consolation and the nearness of God seem to have fled. The one seeking this life must be prepared for this loneliness and solitude, surrounded as it is with the joys and the difficulties of a stable community. At times it may even feel as if the community itself emphasizes our loneliness, partly because we have such expectations of it and for it. Sandra Schneider writes in *New Wineskins*, a book about re-imaging religious life:

> Part of the experience of being human is the ultimate aloneness and loneliness of each of us. Whether celibate or married, none of us can escape the realization of the limits of intimacy, the final ultimate aloneness that even the most intense experience of physical and psychological union cannot obscure or alleviate for more than a fleeting moment. For all of us loneliness must become fruitful solitude or it will become deadly and sterile isolation. Marriage is no guarantee that human loneliness will mature into true solitude; neither is celibacy. But consecrated celibacy is a choice to live that

loneliness in a particularly stark and vibrant way, to drink to the dregs, as it were, the mystery of human aloneness, in the confident hope that the other side of loneliness is union with God. A fulfilled celibate life is a sacrament of human solitude transubstantiated by the love of God into the life-giving bread of human solidarity.

Schneider concludes this challenging and lofty passage by admitting that total success in being such a sacrament is not common-place but remains the ideal:

> It is a rare achievement, perhaps even more rare than the truly sacramental marriage, but both are a splendid gift not only to the church but to the world.[4]

Edith Stein, a convert from Judaism to Catholicism, Carmelite nun and martyr in a Nazi death camp, wrote of the call to universal love as a call to Christian love that applies to all, but in particular to those in religious life consecrated to God. What she calls "natural love" is indeed required for the survival of the race through the physical bond and the care of children, yet lovers and parents are also called beyond the "possession" of others for themselves which is often a bulwark against the loneliness of being alone in the world.

> Natural love aims at possession, at owning the beloved as completely as possible. But anyone who loves with the love of Christ must win others for God instead of himself, as Christ did. [...] Actually, this is the one way to possess someone forever. Whenever we entrust a person to God, we find ourselves united to him (her); whereas, sooner or later, the lust for conquest usually—no, always—ends in loss.[5]

In the vowed life, prayer in its many forms has a priority, truly as relationship to God and others. And in the life of prayer, meditation or contemplation is essential. Contemplation has been described as a standing in the temple of our being, in the "place" where God dwells as our source.[6] It has also been described as simply the prayer of looking and being looked at, rather than thinking or using the mind. It is a prayer of presence and of being with. The contemplative stance is a way of being united to God and to all creation all at once. It is union in faith in God-creator, God-incarnate, God-in-love who is the Spirit. At one with all, we are in solidarity with those suffering as well as with those rejoicing. We are conscious, painfully so, of our being part of the sin of the world. We are conscious of the redeeming act of Christ still among us now in resurrection, and so we are part of the liturgy of the whole world. Contemplation, then, while seeming at first glance to be a lonely thing apart, is in actual fact and practice a uniting, joining act of presence and the *very opposite of loneliness*.

We are not always conscious of the uniting love and presence that is contemplation. There are times when it may seem indeed to be an arid desert. The very God before whom and for whom we are is a mysterious and hidden God. A sister friend of mine who knows this well, yet is committed to a life of contemplation, has expressed it so:

> Why do you think God is silent, Job?
>
> You inexhaustible
>   questionable answer
>   unanswerable question
>
> You Love Question!
>   unquestioning
>
> You alluring
>   tantalizing
>   sideways-looking
>   handwriting
>   in sandwriting
>   Who's Who?
>
> You MAN!
>
> You will never exhaust
>   the mystery
>
> (Emmanuel)

Knowing the desert, both oasis and sand dune, the same writer wrote of that need to reveal ourselves and to be healed:

> i will unwind the bandages on my Nagasaki soul
> i've been through fire and rain
> > alive but not unhurt
> > but not unscathed
> the pieces are here, but i am not whole
> holy? perhaps if you would just
> > be grown enlighten see me
> ...
> it seems i am crumbling around the edges
> > but flowers take root in eroded dust calmly
> > > > (Emmanuel)

A sense of loneliness may indeed be an invitation and a call to a religious vocation. It was so for Sr. Doreen who became a Sister of St. Ann for some years and finally moved further into the contemplative life as a Poor Clare on Vancouver Island.

When I visited the monastery recently and, in the course of conversation, spoke of the writing of this book, Sister Doreen with a knowing smile, said:

"I wrote some pages on loneliness. Would you like to read them? I'll give them to you, if you like."

Of course I wanted to see these pages. I had known Sr. Doreen before she became a Poor Clare and I thought of her not as a lonely person, but as one interested in communication. She fetched the papers. I read them, then asked her if I might include them here. She had written:

> Loneliness has always been part of my life. Even as a child I experienced it. I used to sit by the lake or nestle on a blossoming fruit tree branch, and wonder about what I was feeling. It took a few years before I actually named it, and many more years before I finally accepted it. Now I am not afraid of it.

What were the steps toward that acceptance?

> The stepping stones were: as a child in my alone moments; as a teenager in disappointing relationships with the opposite sex; always in crowds, whether I knew someone or not; in my hunger to be a saint; most

poignantly felt during my year of study (one spends much time alone and thinking when studying); a face to face confrontation with it during my retreat at Berkeley.

This face to face confrontation became a dialogue between Doreen and loneliness.

Doreen: You have been following me around all my life. At first, you were like a stranger to me and would reveal yourself to me at very select times like in my favourite, hidden spots where I used to go to ponder and reflect. I didn't know your name then, but I felt your presence and I was not comfortable with it.

Why did you choose to be my companion when I was still so young?

Loneliness: Oh, I didn't just choose you. It is true that I am present in everyone's life, but some people try to deaden my presence with people, things, travel, work, booze, drugs, pets, sex—you name it. There was a sensitivity in you that caught an awareness and acknowledged my presence. I'm not saying that is negative.

Doreen: But it is pretty hard to consider you as something positive when you cause me so much pain, when you leave me with a depth of emptiness that permeates my soul and causes me to experience insatiable hunger, drives me, at times, to soul-shaking sobs. How can that have even a semblance of the positive?

Loneliness: If you look beyond those feelings and responses you often have, you will see what I mean. Remember the time you stood knee-deep in the calmness of the ocean and held your arms out to the setting sun which shimmered its path along the water to your very feet? You experienced uniqueness in the midst of the beauties of nature. You thanked God for your being, for your uniqueness, for the gift of your life. You experienced then a fullness, a gratefulness for who you were: small and alone. And it was that feeling which came to be coupled with me—loneliness.

Doreen: I remember. It allowed me to experience a oneness with creation which would never have been possible if I had never touched you. And it was there that I specially sensed God.

Loneliness: It is also true that your search to know, love and be united with God has been heightened by my presence. Because you have taken long periods of solitude you have inevitably experienced God's presence in a very powerful way. Do you not think I helped to bring that about?

Doreen: I guess if I'm really honest I have to say "yes." I would never have really understood what it is to be a human being if I had not known you, and I would not have really been able to identify with Jesus, nor understand the concept of Fatherhood—these have been tremendous gifts for me.

I will never forget my deepest encounter with you.

Loneliness: Yes, it was painful but very healing. You finally accepted me, and the fact that I would always be part of your life.

Doreen: It was as if I touched the very core of my being. My acceptance of you and the discovery that you would always be with me regardless of what relationships I had, gave me a new freedom that I had not experienced before.

I know now you are here, I accept you. I am not afraid of you, nor do I try to avoid or escape you. You are part of my very being and I have learned to be at home with you. That somehow makes me feel as if I have discovered something very precious I wish everyone would discover. It is like a hidden part of me which I no longer have to hide or be ashamed of.

Doreen wrote a short postscript to this dialogue:

"In re-reading, I once again felt the extreme relief and healing that took place when I allowed loneliness to be part of me and no longer resisted it."

It would be difficult to distinguish exactly what part of the loneliness Doreen knew was call, what part was the normal loneliness of being human, what part was perhaps the less normal loneliness brought about by upbringing and circumstance; or to what degree, as some people seem to be, she was "born lonely." No matter, Doreen has found her home by walking with that lifelong companion. While loneliness may be an element of a call to community of consecrated life, one cannot seek that life as an escape or to nurse one's rejection of disappointment or failure in life. Such motives could constitute an impediment to the free response of the vows.

It is much more authentic, more normal (and more common!) to be of the mind of Sr. Majella, whom I knew only as an aged sister who loved to tell stories. She used to tell how she "got the call and went off to the convent" even though she was engaged to a minister's son, "a fine man. He loved me and so did his father: I could have married both of them." She would say this with a chuckle and, I hope, some exaggeration for the sake of the story. The point I make is that the loneliness experience in a call to religious life is not a question of being anti-social.

Scriptural consolation

The religious life and the priesthood which involve "celibacy for the sake of the kingdom" (Matthew 19:12; 1 Corinthians 7:7) have great potential for loneliness because they are essentially prophetic in nature. If living the prophetic life is lonely, that loneliness is minor in comparison to the loneliness of being the Messiah!

Jesus was a lone if not a lonely figure. John's gospel says this in the piercing words: "He came to his own and his own did not receive [recognize, acknowledge] him" (1:11). We have seen him struggling alone in the desert. We have seen him rejected by his home town. His was the loneliness of the "guru," the acclaimed teacher, the "rabbi" set apart. We see him often in the gospel off on a mountain or in a garden alone in prayer. He was misunderstood and even perhaps deliberately misinterpreted and, worst of all, identified with evil (Matthew 12).

It was almost as if Jesus did not belong here, even though everything that was made was made through him.

He expressed this loneliness in words such as: "The foxes have their dens and the birds of the air their nests but the Son of Man has no place to lay his head" (Matthew 8:20), and "Who are my mother and brothers and sisters? Those who do the will of God" (Matthew 12:48, 50).

Most poignant of all is the moment when Jesus offers the intimate relationship of union through his body given in the form of bread of thanksgiving. Many walk away. He asks his closest friends, the ones who have been at his side, "Will you also go away?" What must have been the expression on his face, the feeling in his heart? At this point, these "close ones" stood by him, but in the end "the disciples all leaving him fled" (Matthew 26:56).

What did Jesus do with all this loneliness? He socialized with people of all sorts. He gathered people and offered them life, he accepted invitations. Some resulted in deeper friendships, as with Martha, Mary and Lazarus. He invited some into his closer confidence, even though he knew they would not always be trustworthy. He sent them out in two's; he knew it was lonely going alone. He took part in religious celebrations and feast days and he went to the Temple, even though his teaching went beyond the Temple. He kept returning to his centre and his identity as God's Son through prayer to which he committed whole nights. He promised to remain with us so we would never be alone.

Lessening loneliness

- As Weigel suggests, the minister or religious would do well to ask him or herself these hard questions:

What makes me feel lonely?
What do I do when I feel lonely?
What could I change or where could I turn for support?

In the answers to these questions, one might realize that one is resorting to the wrong cures such as: denial, toughness, withdrawal from relationships, dependence on drugs or alcohol, extreme busy-ness, extreme independence, avoidance of prayer.

- Invite together or join a mutual support group that is not a task force only.

- Have a person or group to pray with not just for.

- Delegate responsibilities so as to share burdens as well.

- Set aside times for family, community, friends—without guilt.

- Take time alone for quiet reflection on a regular basis and sufficiently long to become centred and in touch with your being, your purpose, your God.

- Find ways to cut out work and meetings that are unnecessary and de-energizing because you do not believe in their value as real ministry for you or you feel they do not require your presence.

- Every evening, examine the day to recognize God's presence and action in it. Give thanks for the various moments that come to mind. Give thanks for the community to which you belong, of which Jesus is the centre and foundation.

- Admit your weaknesses, your humanness, your need for others.

- Value friendship.

The loneliness of age

This chapter is deliberately titled "The Loneliness of Age" because loneliness pertains not only to old age but to middle age. The loneliness of middle age is not like that of old age but can be just as acute.

The loneliness of middle age

I consider "middle age" to cover a broad span: anywhere from forty to seventy depending on each person's state of health and state of life. In that span of life, much happens to a person physically, emotionally, spiritually. For women who have raised a family, there is the infamous "empty nest" syndrome, especially if no professional career has preceded motherhood or if such a career has been abandoned over many years. Contrary to general opinion, the empty nest syndrome is not confined to women whose "nest" has been abandoned by grown children. There are those who have lived with and cared for parents who eventually die. There are the men whose work has been done with such purpose for the growing family's needs and for whom suddenly an ennui or repetitiousness or sense of being stalled sets in. The crux of all this loneliness rests not so much on "my children have left me" or "my dear ones have gone" as on the feeling, "I am no longer needed." This is devastating, perhaps because underlying that thought lurks: "therefore, I am no longer loved."

On the other hand, it is becoming more common to have to say, "Will my children never leave me, get out on their own? Am I going to be looking after them all my life? And their kids, too?" And then there is the feeling of being used.

Then there are the telltale lines and the greying temples that force us to admit that middle age is on its way: "I'm not as attractive as I used to be." For some women, this can be quite alarming. For some men it becomes the occasion to fall into the trap of resorting to a new love to prove it isn't so.

As if to add insult to injury, there is a "third strike": the terrible, unarticulated feeling that "life is beginning to pass me by," that "I'm in the third quarter and haven't done anything important with my life." And now it's too late! This state of mind has been called "the crisis of the limits."

Even if all the external conditions of family and relationships and work were or are near perfect, the inevitability of hormonal changes ushers us into the next stage of life. In the West, we fight it tooth and nail with medications, denials, facelifts, toupees and what-not—we desperately want to make our second debut as stunning as our first. Yet we experience these body changes and, indeed, ourselves as strange and somewhat unfamiliar. We feel restless and uptight, vaguely disturbed, vaguely disintegrating. We could sink into tears and depression with ease! It is a difficult time, a time of misunderstanding when those closest to us do not realize and cannot really participate in our inner change. It is a time of not quite knowing what is happening to us—a time of built-in loneliness.

A letter from a friend of mine, who is good-humoured and competent, expresses it well:

Today I returned home after a six-day retreat. The theme was, "Who can ascend the mountain of God?" The weather provided all the sound effects for the readings from the Old Testament. We had rain and thunder and lightning and cold for the entire week.

I went to Monticello with a very heavy heart. During the past two months several of my dear ones have passed on or become gravely ill. Selfishly, I resent their departure but I envy them their new life. It is much more difficult to deal with the sufferings of those who are ill and know their time is limited.

Interestingly, for the first time I thought of the possibility of this being my last retreat. I don't think I'm depressed—I just think I'm thinking.

Feelings such as these can be greatly intensified by retirement, particularly for people whose work has practically contained the meaning of their lives. A column in the *UN Secretariat News*, entitled "Fragment of a Diary,"[1] tells the story:

Two weeks ago, one of our colleagues retired and, as often happens, there was a re-organization. The furniture was also moved around and I inherited a different desk. As I was arranging my things into the middle drawer, I noticed a thin notebook half hidden under the last divider. On opening it, I found a single entry on the first page. As I did not recognize the handwriting, and since there was no date, it was not possible to tell how long ago it had been written. I found the fragment rather touching and have reproduced it:

"With three more months before my sixtieth birthday, it seems that I am not the only one who is looking forward to my retirement. Many others are obviously looking forward to it too. I am sure of this, because I have recently noticed that people now look at me differently.

"I am not quite sure what exactly the difference is. Sometimes I think they are seeing beyond me as if I were no longer here... Other times, they seem to be making an extra effort to be nice to me to smooth my exit. But their look has that unseeing quality, as if I have already become a bygone, a non-person.

"I think this explains their effort and their looks. I am already a non-person. It is only out of good manners that they even say good-morning to me.

"I must play their game. I have begun to look forward to see how much further I have moved into oblivion in their minds. The events the past week convince me that I am all but obliterated.

"After an absence of two days, I returned to my office to find that my secretary had been re-assigned, and in her place there sat a stranger. A handwritten note on one of those yellow routine slips on my desk said that unless I wanted my secretary back, Ms. ___ was at my disposal, as if I were a consultant being offered secretarial help. Then yesterday I received a telephone call from a former colleague who is now connected with a university. He wanted to know whether I could let him use my office one day next week for a seminar he is to conduct. I think he was taken aback when I expressed surprise and said that I expected to be in the office all next week and did not see how I could let him use my office. But this was not all. Half an hour later I received a telephone call from a staff member whom I do not know, who said that he had heard that I would be moving and he would be interested in taking over my apartment.

"If I had not already planned my retirement, I might have found all these events rather disturbing. As it is, I am amused. So at coffee today with X, I began to tell him how funny I found these developments. He mumbled something to the effect that I must be imagining things. Then I saw that special look on his face too. I suddenly realized how stupid I was to expect him to understand, for he had not really been listening and in his eyes I saw that he too was seeing beyond the non-person that I had become."

A staff member

All of this being said, we must also admit that we are not forever doomed to this loneliness of middle age. It is a challenging time as well, a time for going deeper into our closest relationships with husband, wife, community, friends, ourselves, God. It is a time to go deeper than the skin or the habits—the mere, undeliberated habits—of life. It is a time to develop in those areas we have had to neglect in earlier years because of work and family responsibilities and in which we may now feel we are deficient. Far from indulging the loneliness, there is time now to indulge the interests, hobbies, even careers we've missed or chosen to set aside. We are just older; we are smarter. And now, it does not really matter if we succeed or fail: no one's life or welfare depends upon it. It is a time to grow culturally, make use of libraries, films, courses. We have a knowledge of living but now a whole world of intellectual and cultural knowledge lies waiting for our exploration. If formerly we studied for our economic advancement, now we may learn for our personal enjoyment. Is this selfish? Not if we realize that the better person we are, the better the world is.

Now is also a time to reach out in volunteer work. There are never enough volunteers for all the services people need. It is a rewarding effort, learning from others while serving them, co-operating with others in order to serve. The greatest among us is the one who serves, as Jesus taught us.

Especially, middle age is a time to develop spiritually, a time to give time to our union with God. It is a time to learn to live at the centre of our reality, a time for a spiritual director because we may need a guide for the new paths opening.

It is a time to examine our lives thus far and to renew our vision or create a new one. Socrates once said: The unexamined life is not worth living. Perhaps the "crisis of the limits" is no more than an invitation to examine our life:

> What can I do that I have not yet done?
> What do I really want to do?
> What do I need to change? to renew? to begin?
> What will I wish I had done at the end of the next "phase"?

We have made choices. We may also feel we were forced into some "choices." Perhaps we feel some of these un-choices are the very cause of our present loneliness. We cannot re-live our lives, and most of us admit we would not really want to do so. We cannot un-make our life choices but we can re-make them.

I once sat at a table over lunch with a group of people, two in their thirties, one in her forties, myself, and an elderly woman in her eighties named Rose. Rose used to help us in the office as a volunteer. At this lunch table, the conversation turned to the question: "If you had it to do over again, would you make the same choices in life?" There was a spirited discussion. It seemed I was the only one who was satisfied with my choices. Rose had said nothing at all but was listening intently. Then she spoke with a sort of urgent distress in her voice: "Children, children, please, do what you really want to do with all your heart and don't have regrets for your life. Don't regret your

life." She was shaking her head as if to say, "How sad!" Rose had foregone marriage and stayed home to look after her aged mother (with very little gratitude from her family) until death left her all alone. Now, besides helping us, Rose went to the airport every Saturday on the bus to spend the afternoon with a mentally handicapped nephew who loved to watch planes. She would take him to supper afterwards. Rose never regretted her difficult choices. Her few words of wisdom stayed with me.

Despite the normal, painful loneliness of middle age, it is a time to claim our lives. We have made it thus far. We have come to where we are and there is a rightness about it. I like to think that I have earned every one of my wrinkles, that I deserve every one of my grey hairs, and I am not about to hide them. I am better than I was twenty years ago. I am happier. But I have been through fire, too, and sprung back up from my own ashes like the phoenix, for the Spirit never abandons us or ceases to create us. "'Twas grace that brought us safe thus far." Send forth your Spirit and renew the face of the earth, my earth. I still have a life to live!

The loneliness of the elderly

The loneliness of the very aged is something of another variety. This loneliness is not temporary. It is the final and lasting loneliness, the very preparation for the final end of all loneliness: the communion of love prepared for us. We shall consider here both the negative and the positive elements of the loneliness of great age. Again, some persons will be more prone to it than others by nature or by circumstance. Still, it has universal qualities... everyone shares this loneliness in old age (even, I suspect, George Burns).

Sister Augustina's story

Sister Augustina is a "senior" sister, frail and elderly, who has just celebrated her Diamond Jubilee as a sister of St. Joseph. I knew that she experiences much loneliness, since she lives in a large house which is nearly empty during the day when the other sisters are going about their work. She was resting in her room after having had a surgical procedure recently. Sister Augustina was always a very active sister, one in fact who could never sit still for long. I asked her what image comes to mind when I say "loneliness." Without hesitation she answered:

"I think of a train whistle or the bells of a train engine leaving the station. When I was very small, we were on our way to Canada from Scotland and we had to wait over in the London train station. Being alone in the dark in a strange city is my image of loneliness. It goes back a long way."

I thought of my own days in boarding school with the train track running by that would have taken me home. All those feelings return at the sound of a train whistle.

I then asked Sister Augustina what words she would use to describe loneliness. And she told me:

"Loneliness is a feeling of fear. But even more it is longing, a vague longing but also a longing to share something with someone—like we are sharing now. Sometimes it is a need at a particular time, while at another time one might even prefer to be alone. As you get older, loneliness is a big thing, one of the biggest. People react differently to it. One person gets crabby. Another can say outright: 'I feel so lonely today. It's so quiet and there's not a soul around.'

"For me sometimes it's a hurt that wasn't so bad yesterday but today has grown out of proportion because I'm lonely. It's like a deferred pain!"

My next question was: "What was your worst moment of loneliness?" She related the experience of her father's death:

"At my father's death—it was 5:30 a.m. and all eight of us and my mother were there. As is the custom of our people at a death, the boys came to the girls of the family, and to mother, and kissed them and they shook hands with their brothers. No one came to me. I think they either thought it was not appropriate because I was a sister in the habit and was kneeling praying for my father, or else they just didn't think I needed it. I felt so left out, as if I didn't belong there. I was excluded. They had put me on a pedestal I didn't want to be on. That terrible feeling recurs sometimes when I'm lonely. I feel excluded. I was never able to talk to them about it. I sometimes have a terrible longing to see my family and a desire to help them. [Her family is out West, which seems to get further and further away as she ages.]

"I pray for them and I am anxious about them. Three have died between Pat and me and the younger sister. Nora is gone. I'm concerned about who is going to go next.

I'm the eldest, but younger ones have gone before me. I think I'd like to go next but then it will cause them pain.

"As for friends, I lost my best girlfriend, a classmate, last Christmas. We've been friends all our lives, for sixty-two years. When I was sent back to Winnipeg, we would get together, and we always wrote to each other when I was here. I miss her so much, just knowing I won't hear from her again or see her. It is really hard to lose your friends."

I had read in an article entitled "The Pain of Loneliness"[2] a quote from Dr. Daniel Russell, a psychologist-researcher:

"It's not that family relations are unimportant to older people. They can turn to family for assistance. But they can have lots of family to assist them, and still feel terribly lonely if they don't have friends. Why?"

Might it not be that we know family may assist us out of duty but friends value us for ourselves? A friend of our own vintage who has given us acceptance, love, and fun, is simply irreplaceable.

Next, I asked Sister Augustina:

"What would you say to people who are lonely, especially if they are elderly?"

Sister Augustina's reply was:

"Sometimes you just sit with them; don't say anything. And also I say to them: Pray. Sometimes when I am pained with loneliness, I just have to go to the chapel. The presence of God there breaks the loneliness. You have to go and do something, go to something. Don't indulge yourself in loneliness. If you feel hurt or lonely, maybe turn on some music. Hurt and loneliness go side by side, I think.

"The older you get, the more you can't go out. It's the big pain. You're afraid to go. A person can't envision this when they are active. You just can't imagine what it's like—and it's here to stay. It is a sort of stripping, preparing us for what is coming. It is important to accept it. I don't always accept it. For example, I have tapes to listen to, stories, books on tape. I can't read any more and that is so hard. I used to read a lot. So even though I have the tapes, it's like I don't really want to listen to them because I don't want to face my blindness.

"You feel as if life is passing you by because it's going too fast for you to keep up. You can't see or hear clearly so you are not sure what's going on. It's a big offering daily. It's a letting go, a dying. People don't remember that you can't see. They leave you a message written on a little piece of paper and are impatient if you didn't get the message.

"They don't ask you to go out any more to a concert or a show because they figure you can't see or walk well enough. You are left out. And people get a bit impatient with you because you miss things. You get out of touch with what is going on in the house. For example, there was a penance service here last night. No one told me about it. It was posted but I couldn't read it so I missed it and I felt so bad. But no one thought to tell me. They don't mean it. And there are those who bring me things or read to me—but one doesn't read loudly enough so I'm not sure I've heard right. It's quite hard. Again you feel left out or left behind. And you can't catch up."

At this point, what Sister Augustina had said of the thoughtfulness of many was confirmed when a teacher, Sister Margaret, knocked on the door and came in cheerfully with a box of Sister Augustina's favourite crackers and some Easter bonbons.

"In a way, I feel all this is for my good because I have to face letting go. And I feel by this loneliness and exclusion I am turning more and more deeply to prayer and it is good. You just give each day to Our Lord."

I was sure that every aging person would relate to what Sister Augustina was experiencing and telling me. I thanked her for sharing the daily pain of loneliness in the aging process. I had not thought of such things as missing what was going on right there in the house because of an inability to read notices. Or missing parts of conversations. I could feel a sort of net of isolation closing in on me. Yet Augustina was quietly trying to accept her lot as well as her physical debilities. She had always kept herself meticulously well-groomed and she said that now, when she looks in the mirror everything is distorted and she is not sure what she looks like. That, too, she has to let go. With all the care and concern and attention one might receive, there would still be the feeling of exclusion and isolation simply because of the failure of one's own faculties to be able to engage with others.

I actually sensed what Sister Augustina was describing in such a way as to feel that perhaps, as I listened, I was receiving a gift of advice and preparation for the time when I too will begin to feel aging and the failure of my senses and of my relationships with others. I told Sister Augustina that I felt her sharing of these experiences, which I could not have described had she not told them to me, would be of real help to many others. Just to know that others are "in the same boat," in that condition of feeling alone and excluded and "shelved," is to be comforted and to share that lonely space with them.

My father

I remembered my father living alone in his house for twelve years after my mother's passing. Most of our family live in other provinces so we tried to stagger visits home and take turns spending summer months with him. On some visits in the late years of his life, I found my father anxious to talk about things that mattered. I believe his faith was tried in those years. He was reading the Bible and, not being a scholar, was struggling with its meaning. When we talked, he would ask me challenging questions, as much as to say, "How can you believe that?" But I sensed he was looking to me to dispel his doubts, strengthen his faith and give him assurance. My father had been a faith-full man, a believer who tried to live out of that faith. He went daily to the church for morning eucharist when he was able. This seeming doubt in what he was experiencing was a trial, I was sure. He weathered it. I admit that I sometimes felt an impatience at his approach because he seemed to be "baiting" me in order to provide a discussion and the answers he sought. But deep down I felt a great compassion for his spiritual suffering and I tried to continue to be responsive and reassuring in my letters to him.

Later, my father suffered strokes. He was able to return home eventually after the first serious one. But these strokes do some damage to the brain. There is some personality change in many cases—a little suspicion toward the one who is doing the most to help. This is common, but when it is one's own father or mother it is very painful. So it was for my sister who did everything she could to enable our father to stay home. For example, when he misplaced something, he would think that perhaps she had removed it. Finally, after a more seriously damaging stroke, it was decided, with much anguishing, that my father should go from the hospital to an extendicare and only then back home, or to my sister's, if that were workable. It was never possible for him to return. He began to fail and it was found that he had a form of leukemia that would take his life in a matter of weeks. But he never unpacked his suitcase; that was a telling sign of his longing to go home. He died a quiet and peaceful death in the presence of his family.

My father's was not an isolated or unusual experience. Numerous elderly people live alone in apartments or houses, wondering how long they can stay yet anxious about an uprooting, that painful cause of so much loneliness. Elderly people fear that once they leave their homes, they will have no more independence, they will not be visited, and they will be treated as non-persons. That is loneliness. While not all families neglect to visit their aged parents or grandparents who are being "looked after" in a home, it does happen often enough to constitute a real fear for the aged. In the extendicare where my father spent his last weeks, one of the nurses remarked to my sister:

"It is so good to see your family here with Mr. Bouchard. Sometimes we call the family when a parent is nearing death or has had a bad turn and they say: Let us know when it is over and we will make arrangements."

A story on this subject, truth or fiction it matters not, appeared in the *Saskatoon Star Phoenix*:[3]

> He had not received a card in the mail—so, they would visit.
>
> It was Grandfather's birthday. He was 79. He got up early, shaved, showered, combed his hair and put on his Sunday best so he would look nice when they came.
>
> He skipped his daily walk to the town café where he had coffee with his cronies. He wanted to be home when they came. He put his porch chair on the sidewalk so he could get a better view of the street when they drove up to help celebrate his birthday.
>
> At noon he got tired but decided to forego his nap so he could be there when they came. Most of the rest of the afternoon he spent near the telephone so he could answer it when they called.
>
> He has five married children, thirteen grandchildren and three great-grandchildren. One son and daughter live within sixteen kilometres of his place. They hadn't visited him for a long time. But today was his birthday and they were sure to come.
>
> At suppertime he left the cake untouched so they could cut it and have dessert with him.
>
> After supper he sat on the porch waiting.
>
> At 8:30 he went to his room to prepare for bed. Before retiring he left a note on the door which read, "Be sure to wake me up when they come."
>
> It was Grandfather's birthday. He was 79.

Such stories are hard to believe. In such cases, everyone loses: the aged person whose end time is approaching, and the family who will one day bitterly regret their behaviour or their failure to be reconciled with a parent for hurts of long ago.

Many elderly people will be heard to remark that they are useless, a burden. Basil who came as an immigrant and worked with our community on our farm for a lifetime—from age 15 to age 75—said to me when I met him at the motherhouse and asked how he was, "Oh, I'm no good any more. I can't work any more." Basil is a living saint! He is one of God's close friends. He knows how to pray. The feeling that "I am no good" is a fact of life for the elderly. They feel "No one wants or needs my advice even though I know that I know some things well."

Women tend to outlive men. As a congregation of women, we have many elderly sisters in our infirmary and motherhouse. Far from being useless, they are our powerhouse of prayer. At our Providence Villa as well, the elderly are there praying and waiting and playing, too. The 97-year-old mother of one of our sisters often remarked, "God has forgotten about me." Even if she really thought so, she had not forgotten him. Not long after suffering a broken hip she was back in chapel—walking!

But one hardly learns to pray only in old age. Prayer requires a long acquaintance with our God along the route. Short of a miracle of grace, which is always possible, prayer, if it has not been a dear and familiar companion of a lifetime, will hardly become our work when we are enfeebled, weary and ill. We all know how difficult it is to concentrate when we are ill, much less pray. But if prayer has been a habit of life, it will be there in us in our aging years, like a medicine against the nagging pain of loneliness.

Positive aspects of aging

It seems that we have found many negative aspects of aging. Are there positive elements as well? Yes.

The elderly have acquired *wisdom*. No matter if it is not asked for or written down: the elderly embody it. In the very being of the aged, life has been lived, an accomplishment no one and no disability can take away. The boat has made the voyage. The aged person has the right to be proud of having steered the craft through waters calm and stormy. That is no small feat.

As for *faith*, that elusive and sometimes derided thing, it is living in the very flesh of the elderly person who has lived by it. The aged are the greatest witnesses of faith, greater than any books or instructors.

Love, too, has found a home in the aged—not the love of sex appeal—but the love of deeds done, of sacrifice, of fidelity to others and to life itself. *Humility* is there, too. It takes a certain humility to allow life to take you through it and not to revolt against "the slings and arrows of outrageous fortune" and "by opposing end them," casting life away.

Teenagers often have a special *relationship* with grandparents or elderly neighbours with whom they can find security and trust, a non-judgmental affection that they may not find anywhere else. To the aging we say: "Only love them for us."

The aged have a powerful *witness* still to give in their dying. The loss of faculties is already a beginning of that process. But dying is an adventure still ahead, to be done poorly or well. It is a journey for which we all need lessons because we are all going to make it, whether we choose to or not. It is the greatest challenge of all—daring to let go.

> The best is yet to be,
> The last of life,
> for which the first was made.[4]

Indian culture, specifically the Hindu, views life as four stages or "ashrams." Each stage is physical, psychological, social and spiritual, each in its own way and degree. First, there is the student life, a time of learning and apprenticeship. Next is the phase of the householder, the person of industry, business, pleasure, family. This stage when fulfilled is followed by the ashram of the forest-dweller, that is, the retirement from the traffic of the world to give priority to the things of the spirit and mind. Finally one enters the fourth ashram and becomes a *sannyasin*, "the one who neither hates nor loves anything," the one who is free. This is the loin cloth stage when even clothes are unnecessary and the person is seen as he is. Most do not reach this stage of detachment, but it is nonetheless symbolically significant.

Each ashram is appropriate to its purpose and is a time to pursue certain goals of human life. The very old in the final ashram are as they are: gentle, integrated, making no excuses, no apologies, having no anxieties and no ambitions, but content to live until the time comes for them to leave the wheel of life. Perhaps we can take a lesson from the Hindu philosophy. Perhaps we put too many conditions on life and fail to relish and respect life itself. When our conditions are not met, we are most agitated and discontent. This is not to deny our human rights but to speak for human freedom in the completion of our lives.

Mary's story

There are some, indeed many, elderly people who are free, living in peace, patient with the fact that it is normal to wear out. They exude a certain joy and make us unaware that aging can be inconvenient! Mary is one of these people.

When I went to visit Mary recently while on a work trip in the West, I did not go to get a story. I just went to see my "ancient" friend who lives alone and is declining in many ways though still alert and lively. She asked me what I was doing these days. I told her about the justice, peace and global education activities that had brought me to the West and then told her that I was writing this book on the loneliness we share. She said to me with a knowing look and smile, "Oh, I know all about that. That's my life."

I waited for Mary to indicate that she wanted to tell me more. And she did:

"But you know, you're never alone. The only one who helped me through was God. If I hadn't had God, I would never have made it.

"I came to Canada on my own, you know. I was only 13 when I went to work on my own."

As she talked, from time to time she would raise her sagging head and try to look at me. The conversation was really a story being told because Mary is totally deaf. Everything I wanted to say to her had to be written on her paper pad. So I listened mostly, nodding for her to go on. I wrote on the pad:

"Why did you come to Canada?"

"I came to get away from an unhappy home. My mother was an alcoholic, you know, Sister. Her brothers would come to visit on weekends and they would fight. I would hide under the bed. My father died when I was very small. I hardly remember him. I worked in a coal mine to support my mother. I had three brothers [she named them]. I lost them all. I was the youngest and the only girl. They needed domestics in Canada. The government paid all the expenses and got you your first job. You paid it back, which I did. I worked in Montreal, Toronto, the Saskatoon School for the Deaf [and now, ironically, Mary is deaf!], Prince Albert—I worked there. Alone on my own all the time. You didn't get to stay with the people you met on the boat.

"I brought my brother over but he took fever and died. Another brother died in Australia and the oldest of pneumonia at home—all in a short time.

"I came further West, worked in a home for handicapped children. I was to be married, Sister. We had received gifts. They gave me a big shower and a party—the matron and staff.

"But he left. I said we must be married by a priest but I also said 'You don't have to become a Catholic unless you want to.' He went away. I never saw him, or heard of him again. I don't think he was married or anything. I felt God had let me down that time.

"I stopped going to church, but the matron—she wasn't a Catholic—she could see something was wrong and she said to me, 'Mary, you go back to your church.' I took her advice and all was better. 100% better. But I had to leave my work there. I loved it, but I had to leave. I told the matron everything reminded me of him, so I had to go. And I did. She understood.

"I got new work. But then the manager got fresh and so I left again. I had some trouble with men, you know.

"The new hospital opened and I was told help was needed. So I applied and was there until I couldn't work any more. I have lived here ever since. I joined the Oblates of St. Benedict. I am consecrated."

Yes, I thought, you *are* consecrated. I had not heard of these Oblates; a seminarian had told her about them and she had written to the Abbot, got the information and joined. This "belonging" meant a great deal to her. I dubbed her also an honorary co-member of the Sisters of St. Joseph. Her bookcases, lining the room, were in turn lined with photographs of her numerous friends, most of them now physically far distant, yet near in spirit and in film. Many of these friends are sisters, all of whom she keeps in touch with by mail. Mary never forgets a birthday or a special feast day. She continued talking about the present:

"I have someone come in on Mondays now to clean for me. I can't do it now. I have friends who take me to church on different days because I can't go alone any more, you know. I am so grateful. Now I can't cook but I eat fruit and I go out for a hot meal at the café nearby.

"I pray for all the needs. Some say it doesn't do any good. I say if that's your attitude, what do you expect?

"Some want to end their life. But I tell them: 'God has given you your life to live and has given you something to do. Talk to God every day. You're never alone because God is right there. Don't think about yourself but about others. Join a group that is doing something worthwhile.'

"People need a lot of love you know. If they have love, they are gentle and kind. If they don't have love, they are violent. I give them lots of love."

I thought of how Peter and John said to the beggar at the Beautiful Gate of the Temple, "Silver and gold I have none, but what I have I give you" (Acts 3:5). What Mary has, she gives bountifully: love. She said she would pray for me too. Then I asked her if I could use her story in the book, since she had experienced tremendous loneliness but had overcome by reaching out to serve and care for others. She replied:

"Well, some people have told me I should write the story of my life but, oh, I couldn't do that. So if it will do anyone some good, you use it."

I asked, "Shall I use your name?" She answered, "Oh, just say 'Mary.' It could be anybody."

Yes, it could be anybody. Mary has identified with everybody, with the human race, in an exceedingly compassionate way. She has not centred on her own loneliness but instead her thoughts are for others in theirs. Her life has been spent in service. Now Mary is all gratitude for the simplest service done for her, for my visit which was not an obligation but a pleasure. I was edified by this aging woman, once so strong, now bent and cut off from the sounds around her. When would I see her again? Perhaps never. But she gave me her story so that I, in turn, might give it to other people, and so, while she sits in silence in her tiny house, Mary will go on reaching out through these few words I have recorded.

Scriptural consolation

In the Hebrew scriptures, our Old Testament, age is considered noble. Old age is considered a blessing. To see one's children's children through many generations was the greatest blessing from God. There were no apologies for staying around too long and no hint of shortening life by "death with dignity." These thoughts would be like throwing the gift of life into the face of the Giver. The fourth commandment, "Honour your father and your mother," carries with it the blessing of long life (Exodus 20:12, Deuteronomy 5:16). The peaceable kingdom described by the prophets always includes "length of days," and the banishment of premature death (Isaiah 46:4). If we walk in the path of God's laws we will have our "youth renewed as the eagle's" (Psalm 103:5)—a welcome prediction for the middle-aged!

Psalm 92 gives a wonderful image of fullness of life even in age:

> The just will flourish like palm trees
> and grow like cedars of Lebanon.
> Planted in the house of the Lord
> they will flourish in the courts of our God,
> still bearing fruit when they are old,
> still full of sap, still green,
> to proclaim that the Lord is just;
> in him, my rock, there is no wrong.

Psalm 71 is the prayer of an old man who declares that God has been his hope whom he has trusted from his youth. He adds:

> Do not reject me now I am old,
> nor desert me now my strength is failing,
> ...
> God, you taught me when I was young,
> and I am still proclaiming your marvels.
> Now that I am old and grey,
> God, do not desert me;
> let me live to tell the rising generation
> about your strength and power,
> about your heavenly righteousness, God.
>
> You have done great things;
> ...
> you will give me life again,
> ...
> prolong my old age, and once more comfort me.

We have also the wonderful stories of Abraham and Sarah, still fruitful in their old age. The children of old age are the children of God's promise: Isaac, Samuel, John the Baptist. Age is a time to give the credit to God since one is aware of one's own diminishing capacities. Nothing prevents God from doing great things in us in our latter years. Age is a time to say with great trust, "My days are in your hand" (Psalm 31:15). It is a time to remember how we have been sustained and cared for through our life, in good times and in bad. It is a time to give thanks for our life. It is a time to remember that we are never alone. It is a time to pray and to believe that:

> The life and death of each of us has its influence on others; if we live, we live for the Lord; and if we die, we die for the Lord, so that alive or dead we belong to the Lord (Romans 14:8).

Whatever we choose to do or not to do, known or unknown to us, has its influence. Who can be lonely surrounded by so many waiting to be touched?

Lessening loneliness

- Accept the stages of life, the "ashrams," the passages.

- Our aging is making room for the next generation. There is a generosity in this.

- To be middle-aged or elderly is a "spiritual task." It is good to have a spiritual director or guide at this time of life.

- Enjoy being grandparents if you have grandchildren. If not, enjoy being an aunt or uncle. Children enliven us.

- Read good books that share people's journeys and give courage. There are some good books on stages of life.[5]

- Keep in touch with friends in parish, community, seniors residence, etc.

- Help yourself without self-pity.

- Dream. You may now be in a position to follow that second career or a modified form of it. Go for it. At this point, you have nothing to lose!

- Give yourself credit for what you have accomplished in life already (for example, you survived, brought up a family, worked hard, etc.).

- If age prevents you from much activity, that does not make you useless. You still have a vocation to love, to witness, to pray, to be. These are the most important and last throughout life. You may be doing all of these best right now.

- If there are reconciliations to be made, do not delay. Long-time estrangements from family or friends make bitter your aging.

- It is normal to feel the crisis of passing into the next stage. All is not lost. Many helpers (medical, spiritual, social or family) can ease and re-assure, as well as help you move on.

- Do the same for others and be patient with yourself.

Friendship and loneliness

I deliberately did not title this chapter: "Friendship Versus Loneliness." We can have good friends and still experience human loneliness. Still, friendship is perhaps the greatest of all antidotes to loneliness. It is one that will never have to come to an end even in eternity, for the kingdom of God is also the fellowship of the saints in light. Friendship is about communication of life among equals and, as such, it reflects more perfectly than anything else on earth perhaps the life of the Trinity. Catherine Doherty, foundress of Friendship Houses and Madonna House Apostolate, goes so far as to say, "The only remedy against loneliness is communication. When we enter the field of communication we enter the field of sanctity."[1]

Egide Van Broeckhoven, SJ

Speaking of friendship for all people of whatever state in life, I would like to introduce a "friend" whom I met through the written word only. He is the late Egide Van Broeckhoven, a Belgian Jesuit. Egide was born in 1933, ordained in 1964, taught high school briefly, and, feeling a strong call, became a "worker-priest" in a factory. He died in a factory accident in 1967. This remarkable young Jesuit left a diary of his spiritual journey and his thoughts on his mission.[2] Some passages from the diary will show why I introduce him in this chapter:

March 2, 1959

> In holy friendship, it is like breaking through the fortifications of a walled city... a friend is waiting inside, deep within the other person.... The true friend is he in whose home one encounters God.

March 4, 1959

> A friend is like a house made of diamonds: within there shines a bright light of great beauty. But one cannot get in without breaking down the outer wall.

Egide later changed his terms about reaching the inner person in a true friendship:

October 24, 1959

> I have spoken elsewhere of breaking down and crossing over walls, in order to penetrate into the inner life of the friend; but this was because my hands and my heart were not pure enough to enter without breaking in....
>
> Light does not break the crystal walls through which it passes. God is light.

But Fr. Van Broeckhoven is not just being fanciful with such images about friendship. He is dead serious about the import of friendship and its meaning.

January 23, 1960

> The apostolate is nothing but the deepest friendship: friendship is the messenger of love from heaven, where we shall be, for one another, the dawn of the innermost depth of divine love.... The apostolate has no other *raison d'être*.

I believe these words bear deep reflection. They may, at first, seem either superficial or heretical. But they are based on the fact of faith, if I may call it that: God dwells within and the centre of every person is in God and reveals God. The young Jesuit writes of transparency between friends, the opposite of secrecy. This self-revelation in trust is also the opposite of loneliness. In this revelation, one sees the face of God. Egide writes:

December 9, 1960

I sought God, I left all things for him, and that is how I found my friend. Now every time I seek my friend, it is God whom I find.

November 10, 1961

My friend is like a city set high on a mountain. I am a pilgrim, climbing toward it.

In the heart of this city there is a temple, built by God and in which he (God) dwells, Trinity of Persons.

If one reflects carefully on the teaching as well as the life of Jesus as portrayed in the gospels, one finds ample grounds for describing the work of the Christian, of the building up of the kingdom of God, as "the apostolate of friendship." It is far from being a selfish or possessive forging of relationships. It is rather entering into a union and a sharing of life, dreams, weaknesses, fears and love that make for fidelity to one's vocation on our way to the eternal banquet to which Christ has invited us in hope and joy. It is a deep innermost sharing of the life of God.

Van Broeckhoven had a deep sense of contemplation and even considered the Carthusian life. Did he have that contemplative loneliness of which Sr. Doreen wrote? And was he seeking to cure human loneliness by friendship of a profound Christian nature? At any rate, he has left us some precious thoughts, including the following addressed to God:

I searched for the inner life of my friend,
    and I found Your inner life;
I looked for what made the love of my friend eternally young,

> and I found You;
> I sought the deepest meaning of the look of my friend,
> > and I found Your face;
> I sought the depth of closeness with my friend,
> > and I found the deepest closeness with You.

One could say that friendship was the life work of this young priest, a work cut off too soon. How could one, with such a life work, be really lonely?

On a practical level, it is quite difficult, when one is lonely, not to be an albatross around the neck of a friend, to leave the other free. A friend must be left free or the relationship will become a burden. The words of the poster say this well:

> If you love something
> very very much
> let it go free.
>
> If it does not come back
> it was never meant
> to be yours.
>
> But if it does,
> Love it forever.

My own touchstone or test for authentic friendship between single people, between celibate persons, between married persons and others of the opposite or same sex is faithfulness: that is, the friendship helps and supports my friend to be faithful in keeping his or her commitments, and me in keeping mine. While remaining faithful, one stands by the other in joy and sorrow. In that criterion is ample room for dying to oneself and living for others, not trying to possess the other, staying free and leaving free, never allowing jealousy to enter, deepening the friendship with Christ of whose friendship the other is a sacrament and sign. In this kind of friendship one discovers both "paschal density" (occasion for much suffering) and tremendous joy.[3]

If the touchstone for authentic friendship is faithfulness to one's life commitments, the safeguard, I believe, is

avoiding secrecy. If the friendship is wholesome, it ought not to be a "covert operation." A good thing wants sharing. If a friendship is secretive, it is in danger of becoming devious. This is not to say, of course, that there are not confidences between friends, but the friendship itself is open.

Examples from experience

Long ago in my teaching career, I met a friend from another school in the course of the inter-school *Pro-Con Forum Debates* held monthly. We were on the same wavelength although we did not always agree. I enjoyed his wit, I respected his intelligence, I liked his style. It was mutual. We teased, we argued, we got serious and we got a lot of work done. While waiting to tally debate results, we tallied up our lives, past and present. We asked each other questions—a lot of questions. We shared our trials, dilemmas, even conscience burdens. We shared laughs, too. We never planned it: it was "serendipity."

For some years we were in touch only at Christmas when I exchanged greetings with him and his lovely family. Then, as always, we met by chance at a lecture to which he came with his wife and I with other friends. It was as if we had been together just yesterday! That is how it is: rare meetings that renew us wholly. We know we could always turn to each other in need. We are both glad each other is alive in this world. The friendship has been good for his marriage, good for my religious life.

I am reminded of another friendship I read about. It was between the author, a married man, and Ita Ford, a Maryknoll sister and one of the martyrs of El Salvador. They had been schoolmates and had maintained a close friendship. Her life ended prematurely and brutally on a dark road in El Salvador on December 2, 1980. He muses in the article (which is more like a meditation made in her presence) on how this death so far away could so affect his life. His wife knows and understands the love of friendship that was there, supporting both this missionary sister and this married family man. It was a beautiful, faith-filled, non-possessive relationship. He could truly feel that he shared her martyrdom. And in sharing the simple story of their friendship, he has made me remember her with a special admiration.

In another experience of friendship that came to my life, the paschal element was more pronounced. The suffering involved was greater, the happiness equally great. During a year of study, I met another friend. It was a personal attraction of shared interests in one of those inexplicable bonds that make one realize that friendship is a gift; the other is simply there, unsought, given. We were a small close-knit student group and formed a community of worship, study and apartment living. Gradually with this particular person a friendship grew that was to be a lasting one. We talked. We walked along the river, both being given to walking. We shared tea after the news each evening. Finally, the year ended and the time came for all of us to go our separate ways. My way was back to the classroom in Toronto. His way was back to the Caribbean. When would I see my friend again? Possibly never.

Spring came. I resumed my work but the separation weighed on me like a bereavement. Distance and absence made the longing to be with my friend not less but greater. One night, I knelt down in the middle of my little room and said, "God, how could you let this happen to me? How can I live like this? What shall I do? You must come to my help. I feel so desolate."

As I knelt down, my desolation began to be dispelled and a realization was given to me, like a dawn. I had what I call a "contemplative insight." All space, time and distance fell away and there was only presence. Everything, everyone, everywhere was present in a union of being. I was flooded with consolation and with the present love of my friend. I felt totally free. Out of that moment came a poem I entitled: "I Hello You Always." One sentence reads:

> Where in the world
> Could you be lost to me?

This love of friendship passed through the throes of selfishness and preoccupation to true, non-possessive, enduring friendship. It was six years after that first parting before I saw him again. We have kept in touch by writing, not often but occasionally. We have been faithful friends: faithful to our life commitments, to our God, to our friendship. This experience helped me to help others in their own throes on the way to authentic, unthreatened and lasting friendship which is a treasure beyond compare.

With another long-time friend of mine, the relationship was such that we could not *not* be friends! That is a gift. I could hide nothing from this friend that I would not hide from myself. He has seen me at my worst and best, as I have seen him. We are able to dispel each other's illusions. One day we tried to recall how we had met but neither of us could remember at all. It was as if we had always known each other. Yet for long periods, we may not see each other more than once a year. But I am not lonely.

In a religious community, itself a very great blessing, there are some with whom one has a deeper, trusting friendship. It is not worked up. It is just there. We are, of course, warned about "particular" friendships, a term for exclusive attachments to one person. These can be destructive to community as well as to the individual because they are exclusive, demanding, preoccupying and in danger of becoming physically sexual. But there are those non-exclusive, non-genital, deeply shared and free friendships that become long-standing and part of the joy and even, I daresay, the stability of religious life and community living. How horrible it would be and how lonely if we were all brother and sister "anonymous" to one another. How sad it would be to have no one in one's community to whom one could turn as a special confidante and friend. Universal love does not mean loving each to the same degree and in the same way.

In friendship within the community, as with others outside it, there is indeed "paschal density." For one thing, we cannot choose whether or not we live in the same house or in different countries, or for how long. Work, community life, prayer fill our days. Good friendships require deep sharing of ourselves in our weakness and in our strength. If we do not allow our friend to share our deepest suffering, we do not trust the friendship. When a friend has suffered with us, the friendship is truly tried and tested. All of this grows in a community whose very existence depends on trusting one another in God and risking our lives together, with Christ as the centre, sharing his Spirit with each and all.

Two "facts" exist about friendship: it is a gift and it has to be worked at. When I say that friendship has to be worked at, I do not mean it can be forced or manipulated. The work is to arrive at freedom and to pass through the sometimes dangerous waters of sexual attraction and jealousy, if one is inclined to these. Jealousy is at heart a lack of trust of both my friend and myself. If I am confident of my own self-worth I will not try to bind the other to me, demanding proofs of loyalty. A jealous friendship is not a bona fide one. Jealousy may well destroy the friendship by turning it into an "affair" or burdening it to the breaking point. This I call the "albatross syndrome"—the weight around the neck. Friendship has to rest somewhere between the albatross and loneliness. It is difficult at times and the possibilities of self-deception or of using people are legion.

One might be tempted to ask, "Is it worth it?" or to say, "I'd rather not get involved, not get that close, not take the risk." That is a choice, but it is a lonely choice. After all, heaven will be the communion of those who love, the fellowship. The vow of chastity is not a vow of preservation but a way of loving. Marriage, too, is a way of loving. Single people, too, need the bonding of friendship to be human. A friend is one for whom we would lay down our lives, as our friend Jesus did for us. I will never forget the first time I experienced that it would cost me nothing to lay down my life for someone I loved. It was a revelation of God's love.

If one *has* a friend, one is not lonely. If one *is* a friend, one is not lonely. A friend is one who calls us forth out of our cocoon, our shell. A friend walks with us when our knees are weak, our feet stumbling, and we in turn walk with our friend. A friend shares our journey and sits at our table and with us recognizes Jesus in the breaking of the bread. A friend will stand at the foot of our cross and encourage us not to come down but to stay there with Jesus until we pass through and are given resurrection. From such friends, loneliness skulks away.

Scriptural consolation

St. Paul enjoins us: "Never be condescending but make real friends with the poor" (Rom 12:16). We are not to think of ourselves, especially we ministers, as being a class apart or above. We need others as much as they need us. Paul says we should make hospitality our special care. In so doing we may indeed find a treasure, a true friend.

Jesus had, even among his close companions, three— Peter, James and John—with whom he shared intimate moments of joy and of agony, as in the Transfiguration and at Gethsemane. He, like us, needed friends to relax with, to share and rest with, as he did with Martha, Mary and Lazarus at their home.

The Book of Sirach (Ecclesiasticus) advises us about friendship:

> Let your acquaintances be many,
>   but your advisers one in a thousand.
> If you want to make a friend, take him on trial,
>   and be in no hurry to trust him;
> for one kind of friend is only so when it suits him
>   but will not stand by you in your day of trouble.
> ...
> A faithful friend is a sure shelter,
>   whoever finds one has found a rare treasure.

> A faithful friend is something beyond price,
>   there is no measuring his worth.
> A faithful friend is the elixir of life,
>   and those who fear the Lord will find one.
> Whoever fears the Lord makes true friends,
>   for as a man is, so is his friend.
>   (Sirach 6:6-8, 14-17)

This passage warns us that one who is not trustworthy and God-fearing (i.e. reverencing God and keeping God's ways) will not find the kind of friend who is also trustworthy and God-fearing. It could be added that one who refuses to reveal oneself, even at the risk of betrayal, will be without friends and will be lonely. Recall how Jesus himself said, "I call you friends, because I have revealed to you everything that my Father has told me" (John 15:15). Jesus, our dearest and closest friend, was both vulnerable and betrayed. But his friendship never failed and he wants us to be with him where he is at the table of fellowship in the kingdom.

In the centuries since these examples from scripture, many saintly friendships are recorded, such as Francis and Clare, Jane Frances de Chantal and Francis de Sales, Teresa of Avila and John of the Cross, Basil and Gregory, Paul and Timothy, Dorothy Day and Peter Maurin. St John Chrysostom wrote:

> A friend is dearer to us than the light of heaven, for it would be better for us that the sun be extinguished than that we be without a friend.

When all is said about cures for loneliness, we will still have our seasons: there will be summers and winters in life. There will be full tide and ebb. There will be waxing and waning as of the moon. There will be silence and communication. There will be death and resurrection: even friendship must be paschal. But may our loneliness be the loneliness we share and not the loneliness of our denial that we are human.

Summary of friendship

• Human beings of whatever walk of life need friendship. Without it life is lonely.

• True and authentic friendship is an experience and revelation of God in the other.

• Secrecy about friendship is to be avoided.

• If we refuse to reveal ourselves and our weakness, we will not have real friendship.

• Those who are faithful to God will find faithful friends, and do well to pray to find them.

• Friendship requires dying to ourselves, to selfishness, and being willing to sacrifice for the friend.

• Friendship is a gift. It also has to be cultivated.

• Criteria for good friendships: inclusive; long term; non-genital; with deep sharing of hopes, fears and weaknesses; free and freeing; non-possessive; supportive of our life commitments.

• Friendship is good medicine for loneliness.

Universal loneliness, universal communion

Must we conclude at this point that loneliness is universal? Is the Universe itself lonely? Certain instances of this come to mind:

- Thomas Gray's famous words in "Elegy Written in a Country Churchyard":

    Full many a flower is born to blush unseen,
    And waste its sweetness on the desert air.

- the mother cat crying for the kittens that have been taken away;
- the horse grazing all alone in a large field;
- the almost mystical silence of stars and planets on a clear night, a silence not unlike the silence of God.

Still, I think the Universe is not lonely for two reasons: First, the Universe "knows" that it is totally, ecologically and mathematically interconnected from the smallest plant in its ecosystem to the stars in their galaxies. Indeed, scientists, searching for the energy behind all energy, have called that energy the "unified field." They conclude that all the processes of nature are but manifestations of different functions of one and the same energy whether as electromagnetism, gravity, the "strong" force that holds things together or the "weak" one that causes decay. The harmony is absolutely wonderful for the continuance of all being and the conditions of living existence.

The second reason is that loneliness requires consciousness, reflective knowledge. With consciousness comes the awareness of separateness and uniqueness as well as desire for union and oneness, both of which are at the heart of loneliness. It seems then to be left to us poor mortals to experience the pain of loneliness; that is, when we forget that we are part of something magnificent, immense, mysterious and much larger than ourselves—the divine project of creation.

Abraham Heschel, the late rabbi and philosopher, teacher and writer, and wonderful, compassionate human being, wrote a book entitled *Man Is Not Alone*, and another called *God in Search of Man*. The rabbi understood well and taught that humans are aware that their meaning and the fullness of their being is beyond themselves, and that they must transcend loneliness and isolation in knowledge, action, artistic expression, and worship. Our awareness of fragmentation and our ideal of union leaves us in the paradox or tension of opposites: routine and spontaneity; mystery and meaning; God's self-disclosure and God's hiddenness; life of reason and life by faith; the misery of being human and the grandeur of humanity.

Heschel raises for us our often felt but seldom articulated questions: Are we alone in the wilderness of time, alone in the Universe? Is there a Presence to live by? Is there a way of living in the Presence? Heschel wrote that the cry for meaning is really a cry for ultimate relationship or for ultimate belonging. These are the very opposite of loneliness. To these questions he answers an assuring "yes." And he goes further to warn us not to turn our search for meaning and belonging into an end in itself, that is, not to pass by the Presence in order to seek and fashion our own private version of being. This is perhaps his way of stating the argument between the existentialists and the essentialists which we discussed earlier (Sartre). It is not so much we who seek God, says Heschel, as God who seeks us. And why does God seek us? In order to make a self-revelation, a self-disclosure so that we may walk together. But we, like Adam, do not want to answer when we are called by name. And who is God? The One who Is. The One who creates, holds in being, knows, loves.

The good rabbi himself was a witness that we are not alone. But the absence of awe and wonder, the end of mystery leave the human alone and alienated because disassociated from the family of being.

But what of the apparent silence of God? It is neither silence nor solitude that makes loneliness, as these poems affirm:

> Silence caresses
> A white rose
> That has no voice
> Of its own
> Save
> That which unfolds
> lovingly
> in
> God
> alone
>
> (Emmanuel)
>
> The Name
> You compel
> my naked feet
> to stand
> alone
> on holy ground
> and calm
> my trembling fear
> in silence.

my trembling fear
in silence.

O blessed
Solitude!

You are
Someone
saying:
"I Am;
that is
who I am."

You are
every Word
that comes
out of
Your mouth.

O sweet
company!
(Emmanuel)

Loneliness in scripture

The word "loneliness" does not occur frequently in the Hebrew and Christian scriptures. These scriptures are much more the story of a people and their God bound together in a covenant relationship. That covenant also bonds the individuals to the people and gives each person identity and a sense of belonging. Nevertheless, we do find the human experience of loneliness and alienation contained in the pages of the Bible. And since St. Paul says the scriptures are written for our consolation and comfort, for our strengthening, let us drink from them and fill our own cup by recalling some of the stories and cries found there and the recorded response of the One who does not leave us alone.

To go back to the beginning, we find it said in Genesis that it is not good for man to be alone. And so a companion, an equal, is made for Adam, the first man. On the other hand, this same couple hides from God because of their disobedience. They do not come out and reveal themselves when called. Thus begins the separation, the alienation and the loneliness.

In contrast, we have many stories of persons answering generously to the calling of their name. Abraham answered, "Here I am," and he became the ancestor of thousands and the Father of Faith. When Moses was called, he answered in the same way. When he was afraid to go alone on his mission, God graciously sent Aaron with him to speak for him. Samuel, too, got up repeatedly at the sound of his name and on the advice of the priest, Eli, replied to the voice that spoke his name, "Speak, Lord, your servant is listening." David was called from the loneliness of the fields where he kept the sheep alone. Later he experienced the loneliness of being rejected by Saul, the king, who pursued him relentlessly. Isaiah, hearing the words: "Whom shall I send?" cried out, "Here I am. Send me."

Many a prophet felt marginalized by the very message he was sent to preach, a message usually rejected together with the bearer. They complained to God about it. Jeremiah had, in fact, decided to abandon his call, but the word burned within him. Who can forget poor Elijah at Horeb, alone, discouraged and wanting to die. He felt he was the only one left faithful to God, so what was the use! But at the word of the Lord, he gets up and goes back to complete his task. He resists the temptation to withdraw and is assured that there are some 7,000 who have not abandoned Yahweh or bowed the knee to Baal.

We can read of the loneliness of those who had a special call such as Ruth who left her homeland to go with her mother-in-law to the land of the Israelites. As a result, she became the ancestor of Jesus. There is Esther in a foreign court speaking for her people who are persecuted because of false accusations. She must approach the king alone, in fear and trembling, but her sense of solidarity with her people enables her to overcome her fear. Then there is Judith going alone to accomplish a terrible task to save her people. Or who could be more lonely than Job whose comforters reproached him and whose wife accused him of some unconfessed guilty deed which incurred his punishment. Not one of them understood. Job at least had the wisdom to acknowledge his ignorance.

Perhaps all these stories can be summed up in the cry of the psalmist. It is a capsule form of the sense of abandonment by God and humankind, the experience of deepest loneliness:

> Yahweh, hear my prayer,
> let my cry for help reach you;
> do not hide your face from me
> when I am in trouble;
> bend down to listen to me,
> when I call, be quick to answer me!
>
> For my days are vanishing like smoke,
> my bones smoldering like logs,
> my heart shriveling like scorched grass
> and my appetite has gone;
> whenever I heave a sigh,
> my bones stick through my skin.
>
> I live in a desert like the pelican,
> in a ruin like the screech owl,
> I stay awake, lamenting
> like a lone bird on the roof;
> ...
> Ashes are the bread I eat,
> what I drink I lace with tears,
> ...
> I am as dry as hay.
>
> (Psalm 102:1-7, 9, 11b)

Yet, at the same time, there are those other beautiful images of the awareness of God's tender presence to his people, images such as taking shelter under the shade of God's wings (Psalm 17, 36, 57, 61, 91) or caressed on God's lap and never being forgotten (Isaiah 49, 66). The cure of loneliness is at least in part to answer when you are called. It is to resist the tendency to sink into self-pity, isolation or withdrawal, even while respecting the need for time to grieve over losses. It is to come out of hiding and to stay with the community, with one's people. And if we do not seem to hear our name called, then we still have to come out and say, "Here I am."

In the New Testament also, we meet persons willing to answer when called, to witness on behalf of God or God's people. Think of Mary, John the Baptist, Peter, John, James, Andrew, Nathaniel, the Samaritan woman, Mary of Magdala, and those countless other men and women who responded to the call and, when it became dangerous to be a Christian, refused to remain in hiding. Leading all these is the response of Jesus, the Son of God, to being sent among us. Truly the Incarnation is God's response to our loneliness. What more is there to say?

The loneliness of Jesus

Let us look more closely at the one who has come to end our alienation, our separation and our deep loneliness. He is the one who did not cling to his equality with God but humbled himself to be like us and with us. "He came to his own and his own did not receive him" (John 1:11). Were ever more lonely words written? He was born in a borrowed stable and died on a borrowed cross. In between, he often experienced rejection or the wrong kind of popularity, from which he fled alone to the hills. And finally, there was that cry of forsakenness that rings in our ears and puzzles our minds, "My God, my God, why have you deserted me?" (Mark 15:34).

How can we ever think that God's own Son did not experience our loneliness or think that we are left alone? Listen:

> I will not leave you orphan; I will come back to you.
>
> (John 14:18)

> Now I am going to the one who sent me. Not one of you has asked, "Where are you going?" Yet you are sad at heart because I have told you this. Still I must tell you the truth: it is for your own good that I am going because unless I go, the Advocate [the Spirit] will not come to you; but if I go, I will send him to you.

The loneliness of the disciples of Jesus

After his return to the God who sent him, Jesus would be with his disciples and followers, with us, in a new and even more intimate way, a way less limited by time and place. He would actually share with us his Spirit who would be as close to us as our very soul. Think how the disciples must have experienced utter loneliness after this loving, brilliant, compassionate, original and endlessly attractive teacher left them. But it was not long before they felt the fire of his love and the breath of his Spirit, the fulfilment of his promise to remain with them until the end of the world. This is the consolation of our faith. Like the apostles and Mary, we must sometimes wait in prayer to know his coming and his presence.

Those same apostles and disciples went out to preach the Good News of God's ever-faithful and saving love, and of God's promise to be with us to the end. At times it must have been difficult to experience rejection and even persecution. We hear Paul complain to Timothy:

> The first time I had to present my defence, there was not a single witness to support me. Every one of them deserted me—may they not be held accountable for it. But the Lord stood by me and gave me power, so that through me the whole message might be proclaimed for all the pagans to hear; so I was rescued from the lion's mouth (2 Timothy 4:16-17).

Still, Paul could write to his trusted friend and fellow apostle. From Timothy and from the churches he had founded, Paul could expect support. Indeed, the result of the befriending by the Holy Spirit of which Jesus had spoken was the bonding of the disciples together into a new people. They formed a community of believers and of life as the Acts describes:

> These remained faithful to the teaching of the apostles, to the brotherhood, to the breaking of bread and to the prayers.

> The many miracles and signs worked through the apostles made a deep impression on everyone.

> The faithful all lived together and owned everything in common; they sold their goods and possessions and shared out the proceeds among themselves according to what each one needed.
>
> They went as a body to the Temple every day but met in their houses for the breaking of bread; they shared their food gladly and generously; they praised God and were looked up to by everyone. Day by day the Lord added to their community those destined to be saved.
>
> (Acts 2: 42-47)

The description is repeated in similar terms in Acts 4:32-37. These pictures of the early Christian community drawn by Luke's pen are the very opposite of loneliness.

The loneliness of Christians today

The same lifestyle is happening in many places today in North and South America, in India, in the Philippines and in other parts of the world where basic ecclesial communities are being formed around the Word of God, the gospel of justice and peace, the sharing of faith, bread and goods. Cooperatives and solidarity in resistance to oppression are making a new society, a new people of hope, though not without suffering. Drop-in centres, support communities for alcoholics, post-psychiatric patients, the homeless and the lonely provide fellowship and a place of gathering and sharing.

The late Dorothy Day, co-founder of the newspaper *Catholic Worker*, wrote:

> We have all known the long loneliness and we have learned that the only solution is love and that love comes with community.[1]

These words, inscribed on her obituary card, express her deep conviction and her life. The community does not consist of a group of perfect people "grooving" together.

In the words of Jean Vanier who also speaks from experience:

> We all carry our own deep wound which is the wound of our loneliness.[...] We cannot accept it until we discern that we are loved by God just as we are and that the Holy Spirit in a mysterious way is living at the Centre of the wound.[2]

If we are all wounded, then we must reach out and help one another. The French writer Charles Péguy says the one who is not a Christian is the one who does not hold out his hand. This definition must at least make us pause and consider. Sometimes, in our loneliness, holding out our hand is the hardest thing of all to do. Yet it is the beginning of the end of our loneliness. It may be simply holding out our hand in response to a hand extended to us. It may be saying "yes" when we feel like saying "leave me alone." It may be staying rather than withdrawing. It may be touching and allowing ourselves to be touched. Jesus touched many, literally, physically, and figuratively, in their heart. One day, we may in turn be able to take the initiative and reach out to another. One day the community may become a communion. After all, do we not share the one loaf which is Christ?

The Letter to the Hebrews gives us good advice:

> Let us be concerned for each other, to stir a response in love and good works. Do not stay away from the meetings of the community, as some do, but encourage each other to go.
>
> (10:24-25)

Paul tells us to not only "do" things for others, but to "be" with them: "Never be condescending but make real friends with the poor. [...] Make hospitality your special care" (Romans 12:13, 16).

Our vocation is to walk through life with one another as pilgrims together. We are Cyreneans, we are Simons carrying one another's cross, which is the cross of Christ, when the weight becomes too great to bear alone. Our communion makes the pilgrimage joyful. This song version of Psalm 16 expresses it well:

> You give marvellous comrades to me,
> The faithful who dwell in your land.
> Those who choose alien gods
> Have chosen an alien band.
>
> For you are my God,
> You alone are my joy.
> Defend me, O Lord.

(John Foley, SJ)

We need one another. None of us can manage alone. Even Moses complained to God: "I am unable to carry this nation by myself alone. The weight is too much for me." So Yahweh had Moses select seventy on whom the Spirit descended: "So they will share with you the burden of this nation and you will no longer have to carry it by yourself" (Numbers 11:14, 17).

Qoheleth, the writer of the book of Ecclesiastes, tells us:

> Better two than one by himself, since thus their work is really profitable. If one should fall, the other helps him up; but woe to the man by himself with no one to help him up when he falls down. Again: they keep warm who sleep two together, but how can a man keep warm alone? Where one alone would be overcome, two will put up resistance; and a three-fold cord is not quickly broken.
>
> (4:9-12)

Still, it seems we must admit that loneliness is a universal experience which even God's Son was not spared. To be who we are—unique, unrepeatable, individual persons—necessitates a sort of terrible loneliness of being. We fear our differentness even while we fight for it! It makes us feel alone. And when we have drawn close and then lose the one who has assuaged our loneliness, what a great loneliness is there! But it is "better to have loved and lost than never to have loved at all."

Finally, there is the coming of death which will abide no threesome. We must go unaccompanied, or so it seems. It must be a lonely passage except... except that one has gone before us and is alive and has promised us life, promised to prepare a place in his home, shared with us his undying Spirit and said he will come again and take us so that where he is, we also may be.

Is there then a cure for loneliness? Yes or no? All things considered, our loneliness is not incurable. We are one with God and with other human beings like ourselves. We are one with the whole universe. Life is a great communion according to God's purpose which has been made known to us in Christ:

> A plan to be carried out in Christ, in the fullness of time, to bring all things into one in him, in the heavens and on earth.
>
> (Ephesians 1:10)

It is for us to be in touch with that plan, to be aware of that communion, to draw together and to act, giving praise and thanks to God for making us in the image of the community and communion of the Trinity.

Notes

Introduction

* *Christopher News Notes*, 12 East 48th St., New York, NY 10017.

Loneliness in general

1   Rollo MAY, *The Courage to Create* (New York: Norton, 1975).
2   Maria GUPE, *Elvis and His Secret* (New York: Dell-Yearling, 1972), pp. 126-27.
3   Ronald ROLHEISER, *The Loneliness Factor* (Denville, NJ: Dimension Books, 1979), p.142.
4   Translated by Babette Deutsch.
5   Martha LEAR, "The Pain of Loneliness," *New York Times Magazine*, Dec. 20, 1987, p. 48.

Being young is not easy

1   Mary Alban BOUCHARD, "Human Story is Everyone's," *Prairie Messenger*, Muenster, Sask., Nov. 9, 1987, p. 9.
2   Kim ZARZOUR, "Picking Up the Pieces," *The Toronto Star*, Oct. 6, 1987. The article, under the heading *Children of Divorce*, mentions agencies such as FIT (Families in Transition) and New Directions. There are doubtless similar organizations in many areas.
3   Mary Alban BOUCHARD, "Entering the Children's Kingdom," *Prairie Messenger*, Muenster, Sask., Mar. 27, 1983, pp. 8-9.
4   Catherine DOHERTY, *Doubts, Loneliness and Rejection* (Staten Island, NY: Alba, 1982), p. 85.
5   Marshall McLUHAN, *verbatim*.

"The loneliness of the long-distance runner"

1   Hubris is the tragic flaw of secret pride which brings about the downfall of the hero or heroine in Greek tragedy, a flaw to which he or she is blind.

2   Rollo MAY, *The Courage to Create*, pp. 28, 31.

3   Vincent VAN GOGH, *The Complete Letters of Vincent van Gogh*, Vol. 4 (Greenwich, CN: New York Graphic Society, 1959), p. 197; quoted in Henri NOUWEN, *The Way of the Heart: Desert Spirituality and Contemporary Ministry* (New York: Seabury, 1981), p. 55.

4   MAY, *op.cit.*, p. 28.

5   Emily CARR, Letter of Nov. 1912, from letters in her own hand displayed at the Emily Carr Gallery, Provincial Archives of British Columbia (Victoria, BC), and brochure.

6   The title of a novel by Thomas Hardy, taken from the 18th-century poem by Thomas GRAY, "Elegy Written in a Country Churchyard."

7   Michael CLARKSON, "Seeking Catcher's Reclusive Author," *Winnipeg Tribune*, Nov. 30, 1979, repeated in *The Sunday Star*, Toronto, Mar. 8, 1981, "Salinger: Still Fleeing the Role of Saviour."

8   Frank KAPPLER, "Dealing with Earthly Hells," *Life*, Autumn 1964, p. 103.

9   Michael J. FARRELL, "Sartre's Bleak Vision: 'Man Can Count on No One but Himself'," *National Catholic Reporter*, May 2, 1980, p. 14.

10   FARRELL, *op.cit.*, quoting Dr. Denis Hickey, Cypress College, Cypress, CA.

The loneliness of culture shock

1   CCVT: Canadian Centre for Victims of Torture, 10 Major St., Toronto, Ontario M5S 2L1. Constituted in 1983, it continues the work of physicians associated with the Canadian Medical Group of Amnesty International.

Bottled loneliness

1   Since I wrote this and even while we sat discussing it, we were interrupted by someone bearing the news that "Irish" had died of a heart attack. He was 46 years old. I felt a sort of loneliness that he would come to our porch no more.

2   William Wilfred CAMPBELL, Canadian poet, *Indian Summer*.

Alienation: The lonely psyche

1   Hannah GREEN, *I Never Promised You a Rose Garden* (New York: Holt, Rhinehart & Winston, 1964).

2   Limited edition published by the author and "Our Place," Toronto.

3   Ann LANDERS, "Suicide Is Never the Right Answer," *The Toronto Star*, Mar. 24, 1988, M4.

4   JULIAN OF NORWICH, *Revelations of Divine Love* (Garden City, NY: Image, 1977), p. 199.

5   John MAIN, *The Moment of Christ* (New York: Crossroad, 1984), pp. 2-3.

6   Institute of Logotherapy: In Canada, contact T. McKillop, 71 Gough Ave., Toronto, Ontario M4K 3N9. In the United States, contact P.O. Box 2852, Saratoga, CA 95070.

7   Viktor E. FRANKL, *Man's Search for Meaning* (New York: Washington Square Press, 1959), p. 186.

8   GROW: In Canada, contact 79 Primrose Cresc., Brampton, Ontario L6Z 1E1. In the United States, contact 403 West Springfield Ave., Champaign, IL 61820.

Dying and living with loneliness

1   *The Sunday Sun*, Toronto, March 1, 1987. First published in *London Daily Mirror*, November 1986.

Sentenced to loneliness

1   Jacobo TIMERMAN, *Prisoner without a Name, Cell without a Number* (New York: Knopf, 1981).

2   Sheila CASSIDY, *The Audacity to Believe* (London: Wm. Collins, 1977).

The loneliness of separation

1   Elie WIESEL, *A Beggar in Jerusalem* (New York: Avon, 1970), pp. 248-49.

2   Bereaved Families of Ontario, 33 Bloor St. East, Suite 210, Toronto, Ontario, Canada M4W 3H1.

3   Regina Mundi Farm, Good Shepherd Sisters, sponsored by Youth Corps, Toronto.

4   Stasia EVASUK, "Group Offers Support to Widows," *The Toronto Star*, Feb. 23, 1987, C3.

5   New Beginnings, Morrow Park, 3377 Bayview Ave., Willowdale, Ont., Canada M2M 3S4.

6   Eugene KENNEDY, *Living with Loneliness* (Chicago: Thomas More Press, 1973), p. 129.

The loneliness of "Religion"

1   Arnold WEIGEL, "Loneliness among Ministers," *PMC—The Practice of Ministry in Canada* (Winfield, BC: Wood Lake Books), Autumn 1986, Vol. 3, No. 4, pp. 15-18.

2   Elizabeth WEBER and Barry WHEATON, "Career Switch," *Compass, A Jesuit Journal*, March 1988.

3   Thomas McKILLOP, *What's Happening to My Life: A Teenage Journey* (New York: Paulist Press, 1986).

4   Sandra SCHNEIDER, *New Wineskins* (New York: Paulist Press, 1986), p. 212.

5   Waltraud HERBSTRITH, *Edith Stein: A Biography* (New York: Harper & Row, 1985). p. 87.

6   John MAIN, *The Moment of Christ*, p. 43.

The loneliness of age

1   ANONYMOUS, "Fragment of a Diary," *UN Secretariat News* (United Nations, New York), Autumn, 1979.

2   "The Pain of Loneliness," *New York Times Magazine*, December 20, 1987.

3   Reprinted with permission of the *Saskatoon Star Phoenix*.

4   Robert BROWNING, *Rabbi Ben Ezra*.

5   For example, Gail SHEEHY, *Passages*, (Toronto: Clarke Irwin, 1976).

Friendship and loneliness

1   Catherine DOHERTY, *Doubts, Loneliness and Rejection* (Staten Island, NY: Alba, 1982), p. 55.

2   Egide VAN BROECKHOVEN, *A Friend to All Men: The Diary of a Worker-Priest* (Denville, NJ: Dimension Books, 1977).

3   Sandra SCHNEIDER, *New Wineskins*, p. 212.

Universal loneliness: Universal communion

1   Dorothy DAY, *The Long Loneliness* (San Francisco: Harper & Row, 1952), p. 286.

2   Jean VANIER, *Community and Growth: On Pilgrimage Together* (New York: Paulist Press, 1979), p. 78.

Bibliography

BOETHIUS. *The Consolation of Philosophy*. Washington: Regnery-Gateway, 1981.

BOROS, Ladislaus. *Meeting God in Man*. New York: Herder & Herder, 1968.

CASSIDY, Sheila. *The Audacity To Believe*. London: Wm. Collins, 1977.

Christopher News Notes. 12 East 48th St., New York, NY 10017.

CLARK, Keith. *An Experience of Celibacy: A Creative Reflection on Intimacy, Loneliness, Sexuality and Commitment*. Notre Dame: Ave Maria Press, 1982.

CLARKSON, Michael. "Seeking Catcher's Reclusive Author," *Winnipeg Tribune*, Nov. 30, 1977; *Toronto Star*, Mar. 18, 1981.

DAY, Dorothy. *The Long Loneliness*. San Francisco: Harper & Row, 1952.

DELESPESSE, Max. *The Church Community: Leaven and Lifestyle*. Ottawa: St. Paul University, 1968.

Divorced Catholic's Credo. The Canadian Association of Separated and Divorced Catholics, 830 Bathurst St., Toronto, ON M5R 3G1.

DOHERTY, Catherine. *Doubts, Loneliness and Rejection*. Staten Island, NY: Alba, 1982.

FARRELL, Michael. "Sartre's Bleak Vision," *National Catholic Reporter*, Kansas City, MO, May 2, 1980, p. 14.

FINDLEY, Timothy. *Not Wanted on the Voyage*. New York: Delacorte, 1985.

FRANKL, Viktor. *Man's Search for Meaning*. New York: Washington Square Press, 1959.

GLASSER, William. *Reality Therapy: A New Approach to Psychiatry*. San Francisco: Harper & Row, 1975.

GREEN, Hannah. *I Never Promised You a Rose Garden*. New York: Holt, Rhinehart and Winston, 1964.

GUPE, Maria. *Elvis and His Secret*. Translated by Sheila La Forge. New York: Dell-Yearling, 1972.

HERBSTRITH, Waltraud. *Edith Stein: A Biography*. New York: Harper & Row, 1985.

HESCHEL, Abraham. *Man Is Not Alone: A Philosophy of Judaism*. New York: Farrar, Straus & Giroux, 1976.

———. *Man's Quest for God: Studies in Prayer and Symbolism*. New York: Scribner, 1981.

———. *Quest for God: A Journey into Prayer and Symbolism*. New York: Crossroad, 1982.

HILLESUM, Etty. *An Interrupted Life: The Diaries of Etty Hillesum 1941-43*. New York: Washington Square Press, 1981.

KAPPLER, Frank. "Dealing with Earthly Hells," *Life*, 1964, month not recorded.

KENNEDY, Eugene. *Living with Loneliness*. Chicago: Thomas More Press, 1973.

———. *Loneliness and Everyday Problems*. Garden City, NY: Doubleday, 1983.

KÜBLER-ROSS, Elizabeth. *On Death and Dying*. New York: Macmillan, 1970.

——— and M. WARSHAW. *AIDS: The Ultimate Challenge*. New York: Macmillan, 1987.

———. *Death: The Final Stage of Growth*. Englewood, NJ: Prentice-Hall, 1975.

LEAR, Martha. "The Pain of Loneliness," *The New York Times Magazine*, Dec. 20, 1987, pp. 47-48.

LEWIS, C.S. *A Grief Observed*. San Francisco: Harper & Row, 1963.

MAIN, John. *The Moment of Christ*. New York: Crossroad, 1984.

MAY, Rollo. *The Courage to Create*. New York: Norton, 1975.

———. *Love and Will*. New York: Dell, 1974.

———. *Man's Search for Himself*. New York: Dell, 1973.

McKILLOP, Thomas. *What's Happening to My Life: A Teenage Journey*. New York: Paulist Press, 1986.

———. *What It's All About: Youth in Search of Meaning*. Burlington: Trinity Pbns., 1988.

MOUSTAKAS, Clark E. *Loneliness*. Englewood Cliffs: Prentice-Hall, 1961.

O'BRIEN, Liam. *The Friendly Way to Mental Health*. c/o GROW Canada, 79 Primrose Cresc., Brampton, ON L6Z 1E1.

REISMAN, David. *The Lonely Crowd: A Study of the Changing American Character*. New Haven: Yale University Press, 1973.

RIPPLE, Paula. *Called to Be Friends*. Notre Dame: Ave Maria Press, 1980.

———. *Walking with Loneliness*. Notre Dame: Ave Maria Press, 1982.

ROLHEISER, Ronald. *The Loneliness Factor*. Denville: Dimension Books, 1979.

SCHNEIDER, Sandra. *New Wineskins*. New York: Paulist Press, 1986.

SHEEHY, Gail. *Passages: Predictable Crises of Adult Life*. Toronto: Clarke Irwin, 1976.

SILLITOE, Alan. *The Loneliness of the Long-Distance Runner*. New York: Signet, 1971.

STEIN, Edith. *Life in a Jewish Family 1891-1916: An Autobiography*. Translated by Koeppel. Washington: ICS Pbns., 1986.

TIMERMAN, Jacobo. *Prisoner without a Name, Cell without a Number*. Translated by T. Talbot. New York: Knopf, 1981.

VAN BROECKHOVEN, Egide. *A Friend to All Men: The Diary of a Worker-Priest*. Translated by T. Matus. Denville: Dimension, 1977.

VANIER, Jean. *Community and Growth: On Pilgrimage Together*. Translated by Ann Shearer. New York: Paulist Press, 1979.

WEBER, Elizabeth and Barry WHEATON. "Career Switch," *Compass*, Toronto, 10 St. Mary St., Toronto, ON March, 1988.

WEIGEL, Arnold. "Loneliness among Ministers," *PMC—The Practice of Ministry in Canada*, Winfield, B.C., Autumn 1986, vol. 3, No. 4.

WIESEL, Elie. *A Beggar in Jerusalem*. New York: Avon, 1970.

150 Copy 2
BDU

Printed in Canada